Study Guide for Richard A. Lippa's

Introduction to Social Psychology

GARY S. NICKELL
Moorhead State University

Wadsworth Publishing Company
Belmont, California
A Division of Wadsworth, Inc.

ISBN 0-534-11773-2

Printed in the United States of America   49

1 2 3 4 5 6 7 8 9 10—94 93 92 91 90

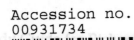

Studying... ...ipa's

Introduction to

Social Psychology

CONTENTS

INTRODUCTION: HOW TO USE YOUR STUDY GUIDE

Welcome to the world of social psychology. This study guide is designed to assist you in learning and mastering the material presented in Richard Lippa's INTRODUCTION TO SOCIAL PSYCHOLOGY. The study guide is organized into six sections: chapter outline, learning objectives, key terms to know, completion items, matching terms and concepts, and multiple choice questions.

Although there are many methods for learning this material, a method known as the "SQ3R" system is a proven way to effectively learn and study.* SQ3R is an acronym for the five steps in this method: survey, question, read, recite, and review.

Step one is to **"survey"** the material. The **outline** and **learning objectives** in the beginning of each chapter in the study guide and the **summary** at the end of each chapter in the text should give you an overall look at the material that needs to be learned.

Step two is to ask yourself **"questions"** about the material as you read the text. Lippa assists you in this process by providing a number of questions throughout each chapter. These questions are designed to stimulate critical thinking and lead you to relevant conclusions.

Step three is to **"read"** actively each chapter, usually one section at a time. Underline or highlight important key terms and the main points as you read along. Pay particular attention to the figures and tables in the text.

---

* Robinson, R. P. (1970). Effective study (4th ed.). New York: Harper & Row.

Step four is to **"recite"** the key points.
When you recite you are actively rehearsing the
material. You can recite the material silently,
aloud, or by taking notes.

Step five is a **"review"** of the material.
The study guide can be very useful in the review
process. Reading the chapter summary and chapter
objectives and key terms in the study guide is a
good starting point. The learning objectives and
key terms are page-referenced to the text.

The completion items, matching terms and
concepts, and multiple choice questions provide a
way to test your comprehension of the material
and may reveal the need for additional review.
The "answer keys" at the end of each chapter give
the correct responses.

CHAPTER 1

WHAT IS SOCIAL PSYCHOLOGY?

CHAPTER OUTLINE

I. The Nature of Social Psychology

    A. Social Psychology Studies Influences on Social Behavior
    B. Social Psychology Explains Social Behavior
       1. Levels of explanation
    C. Social Psychology Studies Social Behavior
    D. The Self in Social Psychology
    E. Differences Between Social Psychology and Related fields

II. Theories in Social Psychology

    A. The Functions of Social Psychological Theories
       1. Theories explain and predict social behavior
       2. Theories help organize empirical findings
       3. Theories focus and direct research
    B. Four Theoretical Perspectives
       1. Learning theories
       2. Cognitive consistency theories
       3. Attribution and other cognitive information-processing theories
       4. Equity and exchange theories

III. Applying Social Psychology

    A. The Two Faces of Applied Social Psychology
    B. The Profession of Social Psychology

IV. Summary

V. <u>Glossary</u>

LEARNING OBJECTIVES

After reading and studying Chapter 1, you should be able to answer the following questions.

1. Give several examples of questions that social psychologists might ask when trying to understand real-world events. (3-5)

2. Define social psychology. (6)

3. Which of the many ways of explaining behavior are emphasized in social psychology? (6-9)

4. Identify several differences between social psychology and other related fields. (11-12)

5. Describe the three major functions of theory in social psychology. (11-13)

6. List and briefly describe the four major theoretical approaches in social psychology. (13-17)

7. Describe the two aspects of applied social psychology. (17-18)

KEY TERMS TO KNOW

After reading and studying Chapter 1, you should be able to define or understand the following terms.

social psychology (6)
social group (6)
mediating variables (8)
attitudes (9)
emotions (9)

COMPLETION ITEMS

Fill in the word(s) to complete each of the following statements. Check your responses against the correct answers at the end of this chapter.

1. Social psychology studies how _____ influence people.

2. Many topics central to social psychology deal with the influence of current _____ _____ on individuals' behavior.

3. The "_____," or the self as an object of knowledge and contemplation, consists of all the knowledge each of us has about ourselves.

4. Social psychological theories provide systematic ways of explaining and predicting _____ behavior.

5. _____ theories focus on how classical conditioning, operant conditioning, and modeling can be applied to social behavior.

6. The _____ of_____ holds that if someone does us a favor, we should be willing to do a favor in return.

7. Social psychology represents an attempt to understand and explain how the _____, _____, and _____ of individuals are influenced by the actual, imagined, or implied presence of others

8. Social psychology is a combination of _____ and _____ science.

9. _____ theory focuses on the consistency and inconsistency of our likes and dislikes.

10. _____ traits are stable dispositions that influence broad domains of behavior.

MATCHING TERMS AND CONCEPTS

Write the letter of the term or concept from below that best fits the following phrases or sentences. Check your responses against the correct answers at the end of this chapter.

____ 1. People strive for consistency among their beliefs and feelings.

____ 2. Human interactions are governed by their costs, rewards, and profits.

____ 3. People strive to understand the world around them.

____ 4. If someone does us a favor, we should be willing to do them a favor in return.

____ 5. Research that focuses on real-life events

a. learning theories
b. equity and exchange theories
c. cognitive-consistency theories
d. norm of reciprocity
e. attribution theories
f. applied science

MULTIPLE CHOICE QUESTIONS

Circle the one best answer to each question.
Check your responses against the correct answers
at the end of this chapter.

1. The majority of social psychologists with
   Ph.D.'s work
   a. in business and government settings
   b. in human service fields
   c. at colleges and universities
   d. none of the above

2. _____ are transient states of arousal and
   cognitions that motivate and direct behavior.
   a. Emotions
   b. Attitudes
   c. Personality traits
   d. Mediating variables

3. The major function of theories is
   a. to explain and predict social behavior
   b. to help organize empirical findings
   c. to focus and direct research
   d. all of the above

4. ____ theory suggests that when people hold
   inconsistent beliefs they experience an
   uncomfortable motivational state.
   a. Learning
   b. Cognitive dissonance
   c. Equity
   d. Attribution

5. _____ theories have been applied most directly to how we perceive and remember information about other people.
   a. Cognitive
   b. Learning
   c. Exchange
   d. Consistency

6. Explanatory variables that cannot be directly observed but must be inferred from behavior are called _____ variables.
   a. independent
   b. mediating
   c. dependent
   d. control

7. In 1890, _____ proposed that "the self" is made up of two aspects, the "me" and the "I."
   a. Sigmund Freud
   b. William James
   c. Ivan Pavlov
   d. B. F. Skinner

8. Modern social psychology tends to favor _____ theories in explaining and predicting aspects of social behavior.
   a. grand unitary
   b. very old
   c. middle-range
   d. narrow-based

9. In comparison to other social scientists, social psychologists are more likely to focus on _____ as the unit of analysis.
   a. society
   b. culture
   c. social class
   d. the individual

ANSWERS TO COMPLETION ITEMS

 1. people   (6)
 2. situational pressures   (8)
 3. me   (10)
 4. social   (12)
 5. Learning   (13)
 6. norm of reciprocity   (16)
 7. thoughts; feelings; behaviors   (6)
 8. pure; applied   (17-18)
 9. Balance   (15)
10. Personality   (9)

ANSWERS TO MATCHING QUESTIONS

 1. c   (13-15)
 2. b   (14-17)
 3. e   (14-15)
 4. d   (16)
 5. f   (17-18)

ANSWERS TO MULTIPLE CHOICE QUESTIONS

 1. c   (19)
 2. a   (9)
 3. d   (12-13)
 4. b   (13-14)
 5. a   (15)
 6. b   (7-9)
 7. b   (10)
 8. c   (11)
 9. d   (11)

CHAPTER 2

SOCIAL PSYCHOLOGICAL RESEARCH

CHAPTER OUTLINE

I.   Issues in Social Psychological Research

    A. Theories in Social Psychology
    B. Operational Definitions in Social Psychology
    C. Reliability and Validity of Measures
    D. Kinds of Social Psychological Studies
       1. Experiments
       2. Correlational studies
       3. Quasi-experimental designs
    E. Generalizing from the Results of Research Studies
       1. Laboratory versus field studies
       2. Internal and external validity
       3. Replication
       4. The issue of realism
       5. Combining the results of many studies
    F. Statistics and Social Psychological Research
       1. Significance levels
       2. The mean and median
       3. Correlation coefficients
    G. Bias in Social Psychological Research
       1. Experimenter bias
       2. Subject bias

II. Ethics in Social Psychological Research

    A. Ethical Problems
    B. Measures to Reduce Ethical Problems -- APA Guidelines
       1. Peer review
       2. Informed consent
       3. Debriefing

III. The Social Relevance of Social
     Psychological Research

IV. Summary

V. Glossary

LEARNING OBJECTIVES

After reading and studying Chapter 2, you should
be able to answer the following questions.

1. What are the two types of operational
   definitions? Give an example of each.
   (27-29)

2. Describe the research method used by Stanley
   Milgram in his studies of obedience. What
   were some of the results obtained in his
   initial studies? (22-25)

3. How are theories in social psychology tested
   scientifically? (26-28)

4. What is the difference between reliability
   and validity? (29)

5. Discuss the essential elements of an
   experiment. (30-33)

6. Explain the purpose of random assignment of
   subjects in an experiment. (30-33)

7. What are the major advantages and
   disadvantages of experimental studies and
   correlational studies? What information is
   provided by experimental and correlational
   studies? (30-36)

8. What is a quasi-experimental design? What are its advantages and disadvantages? (36-37)

9. Discuss the advantages and disadvantages of laboratory versus field studies. (36-39)

10. What is internal and external validity? (39)

11. List and briefly discuss the three forms of replication. (39-42)

12. What are the two different types of realism? (40)

13. What is the purpose of statistics in social psychological research? What does statistical significance mean? (43-45)

14. What is the meaning of positive, negative, and zero correlations? What do correlation coefficients signify? (44-46)

15. What is meant by experimenter bias? How can it be minimized? How is it different from subject bias? (47-49)

16. What are some of the ethical principles psychologists are expected to observe when conducting research on human subjects? (52)

17. What are some of the measures or techniques that are used to reduce ethical problems in psychological research? (52-54)

KEY TERMS TO KNOW

After reading and studying Chapter 2, you should be able to define or understand the following terms.

COMPLETION ITEMS

Fill in the word(s) to complete each of the following statements. Check your responses against the correct answers at the end of this chapter.

1. In Milgram's experiment, subjects were asked to give increasingly higher levels of _____ _____ upon command from a(n) _____.

2. _____ are sets of propositions that are used to explain, predict, and organize _____ data.

3. The two types of operational definitions are _____ reports and _____ measures.

4. A(n) _____ measure is repeatable and consistently obtained. A(n) _____ measure assesses what it is designed to measure.

5. Social psychological studies usually come in two forms: _____ and _____ studies.

6. In an experiment, the _____ group does not receive the experimental treatment.

7. In a(n) _____ study, there is a manipulation of an independent variable but there is no truly random assignment of subjects.

8. Two variables are said to be _____ when they occur together and it is impossible to tell whether an experimental effect is due to one or the other variable.

9. Traditionally, social psychology has emphasized _____ experiments.

10. Experiments show _____ relationships between two variables; correlational studies can show only that two variables are _____.

MATCHING TERMS AND CONCEPTS

Write the letter of the term or concept from below that best fits the following phrases or sentences. Check your responses against the correct answers at the end of this chapter.

____ 1. Variable that the researcher manipulates or intentionally varies

____ 2. Experiments done in natural, real-life settings

____ 3. Refers to how well a study approximates real-life settings and behavior

____ 4. A statistical technique that combines the results of many studies to determine if the results are reliable

____ 5. The branch of statistics that deals with making inferences from data and testing hypotheses

____ 6. The statistical measure of how much two variables are related or "go together"

____ 7. Variable that results from the manipulation in an experiment

____ 8. When the results are sufficiently unlikely to be due to chance

a. mundane realism
b. experimental realism
c. independent variable
d. dependent variable

e. field experiments
f. correlation coefficient
g. inferential statistics
h. meta-analysis
i. statistical significance

MULTIPLE CHOICE QUESTIONS

Circle the one best answer to each question.
Check your responses against the correct answers
at the end of this chapter.

1. A(n) _____ definition is a definition of
   some concept in terms of the procedures or
   methods used to measure the concept.
   a. empirical
   b. operational
   c. theoretical
   d. hypothetical

2. Useful theories typically are
   a. logically consistent
   b. relatively simple
   c. capable of being disproved
   d. all of the above

3. In an experiment, the researcher
   intentionally manipulates or varies the
   _____ variable.
   a. control
   b. independent
   c. dependent
   d. confounding

4. Random assignment is an essential element of
   an experiment in order to
   a. rule out other extraneous variables
   b. determine the level of significance
   c generalize to a larger population
   d. develop a hypothesis

5. In comparison to experimental studies, one of the major disadvantages of correlational studies is that they
   a. may be artificial
   b. cannot demonstrate cause-effect relations
   c. lack realism
   d. must be done in the laboratory

6. An experiment has _____ when its findings can be generalized to other settings and populations.
   a. internal validity
   b. external validity
   c. reliability
   d. naturalness

7. A(n)_____ replication tries to extend the results of the original study by including new variables or conditions.
   a. exact
   b. conceptual
   c. systematic
   d. none of the above

8. Providing information to subjects before they participate so that they may decide whether to take part in the study is an ethical principle called
   a. debriefing
   b. informed consent
   c. peer review
   d. deception

9. In the study in which nurses were ordered by a doctor to administer an obviously dangerous overdose of a drug to a patient, _____ of the nurses began to carry out the doctor's orders.
   a. none   c. about half
   b. few   d. almost all

10. _____ occurs when experimenters inappropriately communicate their hypotheses to subjects.
a. Experimenter bias
b. Subject bias
c. Systematic bias
d. Mundane realism

11. The more often you go to class, the higher your score on an exam. This is an example of a(n) ____ correlation.
a. zero
b. positive
c. negative
d. experimental

12. Problems caused by demand characteristics can be reduced by the use of
a. nonreactive measures
b. field experiments
c. trained subjects
d. behavioral measures

13. Ethical problems can be reduced through the use of
a. peer review
b. informed consent
c. professional guidelines
d. all of the above

14. Which research method has the advantage of having the greatest degree of control?
a. experimental
b. quasi-experimental
c. correlational
d. field studies

15. In _____ experiments, the experimenter does not know which experimental condition the subject is in.
a. blind
b. field
c. laboratory
d. quasi-experimental

ANSWERS TO COMPLETION ITEMS

1. electrical shock; experimenter (23-25)
2. Theories; empirical (25)
3. subjective; behavioral (27)
4. reliable; valid (29)
5. experiments; correlational (29)
6. control (31)
7. quasi-experimental (36)
8. confounded (39)
9. laboratory (39)
10. cause-effect; related (34)

ANSWERS TO MATCHING QUESTIONS

1. c (30)
2. e (36-37)
3. a (40)
4. h (43)

5. g (43)
6. f (44)
7. d (30)
8. i (43-44)

ANSWERS TO MULTIPLE CHOICE QUESTIONS

1. b (27)
2. d (27)
3. b (30)
4. a (30-32)
5. b (33-37)
6. b (39)
7. c (40)
8. b (53)
9. d (41)
10. a (47)
11. b (44-46)
12. a (49)
13. d (52-53)
14. a (37)
15. a (48)

CHAPTER 3

PERSON PERCEPTION

CHAPTER OUTLINE

I. <u>Introduction to Person Perception</u>

    A. The Nature of Person Perception
    B. Difference Between Person Perception and Object Perception
    C. Research Topics in Person Perception
       1. Direct judgments
       2. Attribution
       3. Social cognition

II. <u>First Impressions</u>

    A. Physical Characteristics
    B. Nonverbal Behaviors
       1. The significance of nonverbal information
       2. Kinds of nonverbal behavior
       3. Nonverbal behavior, power, and preference
    C. The Power of First Impressions
       1. The primacy effect and personality judgments
       2. The primacy effect and judgments of ability

III. <u>Accuracy of Direct Judgments</u>

    A. Judging Personality
       1. Early research and problems with statistical measures of accuracy
       2. New directions in accuracy research
       3. Dimensions of perceived personality
    B. Judging Emotions
       1. Darwin's legacy
       2. Recent research

　　　　3. Cross-cultural universality
　　　　4. Facial scoring systems
　　　C. Detection Deception
　　　　1. Nonverbal cues of deception
　　　　2. Vocal cues of deception
　　　　3. Actual versus perceived cues of deception
　　　　4. Detecting deception in real life

IV. <u>Direct Judgments: A Postscript</u>

V.　<u>Summary</u>

VI. <u>Glossary</u>

LEARNING OBJECTIVES

After reading and studying Chapter 3, you should be able to answer the following questions.

1. What is meant by the concept of person perception?　(61)

2. How does person perception differ from object perception?　(62-63)

3. What are the three general research topics studied in research on person perception?　(63-64)

4. What physical characteristics have a major influence on our first impressions?　(65-66)

5. List and briefly describe the five kinds of nonverbal behaviors.　(67-68)

6. Discuss the relationship between nonverbal behavior and information about power and intimacy.　(68-69)

7. Describe the influence of first impressions in the courtroom. (70-71)

8. What are the primacy and recency effects? (71-73)

9. Discuss some of the factors that affect the accuracy of personality judgments. (73-78)

10. According to research by Rosenberg and associates (1968), what two basic dimensions underlie our impressions of others? (78-79)

11. Describe the influence of Charles Darwin's theories on our judgment of emotion. (79-81)

12. What are the six primary emotions that humans can accurately recognize? (81)

13. What does the evidence suggest concerning whether the expression and recognition of emotions are universal across cultures? (81-84)

14. How accurate are people at detecting deception? Are Customs officers better than lay people at detecting deception? (86-93)

15. What kinds of cues (body and vocal) reveal deception more accurately than others? (87-89)

KEY TERMS TO KNOW

After reading and studying Chapter 3, you should be able to define or understand the following terms.

person perception (61)
object perception (61-62)
causal agents (62)

COMPLETION ITEMS

Fill in the word(s) to complete each of the
following statements. Check your responses
against the correct answers at the end of this
chapter.

1. _____ perception is more susceptible
   than _____ perception to errors and
   biases.

2. _____ refers to status and dominance in social life, whereas _____ refers to our degree of liking for or intimacy with others.

3. _____ argued that emotional expressions evolved because of their survival value.

4. People more accurately detect deception from a combination of _____ and _____ cues.

5. _____ are conscious, self-directing entities possessing wishes, motives, and intentions.

6. First _____ are often based on physical appearance and nonverbal behavior.

7. _____ are self-directed gestures that occur when a person is not paying attention to himself or herself, or is distracted.

8. The three main nonverbal behaviors associated with power and intimacy are _____, _____, and _____.

9. The two main dimensions that underlie our impressions of others are good versus bad _____ traits and good versus bad _____ traits.

10. Recent research suggests that the recognition and display of primary facial emotions is _____ across cultures.

MATCHING TERMS AND CONCEPTS

Write the letter of the term or concept from below that best fits the following phrases or sentences. Check your responses against the correct answers at the end of this chapter.

____ 1. How we infer the causes of behavior

____ 2. How we store, combine, and process information about others

____ 3. How we arrive at first impressions

____ 4. The first information carries more weight than later information.

____ 5. Refers to cultural norms that govern emotional expressions

____ 6. A pretrial interview of prospective jurors

a. display rules
b. direct judgment
c. primacy effect
d. voir dire
e. attributions
f. social cognitions

MULTIPLE CHOICE QUESTIONS

Circle the one best answer to each question. Check your responses against the correct answers at the end of this chapter.

1. _____ is the process by which we judge the traits and characteristics of others.
   a. Impression management c. Social cognition
   b. Person perception   d. Object perception

2. The results from the study by Rosenthal and Jacobson (1968) in which teachers were led to believe that some of their students were bright "late bloomers" indicate that compared to a control group
   a. both the "late bloomers" and the control children improved their performance
   b. the student labeled as "late bloomers" showed decline in performance
   c. the student labeled as "late bloomers" performed better on an achievement test.
   d. none of the above

3. Nonverbal gestures that carry a specific meaning within a specific culture are known as
   a. emblems   c. regulators
   b. illustrators   d. adaptors

4. People tend to weigh _____ information more heavily in developing their impressions of others.
   a. verbal   c. consistent
   b. nonverbal   d. written

5. Which of the following is most likely to influence our first impression of another person?
   a. physical characteristics
   b. reputation
   c. personality
   d. verbal skills

6. People who rate themselves as liberal are likely to overestimate the number of other people who are liberal. This tendency is called the
   a. central trait theory
   b. primacy effect
   c. response set effect
   d. false consensus effect

7. Research suggests that most people can accurately recognize ____ on the basis of facial expressions alone.
   a. two basic emotions
   b. six primary emotions
   c. only joy, fear, and sadness
   d. anger, but not disgust

8. The nonverbal qualities of speech such as tone of voice are called
   a. paralinguistic cues
   b. display cues
   c. illustrators
   d. adaptors

9. Research suggests that people are _____ at detecting deception in others.
   a. very accurate
   b. very inaccurate (10% of the time)
   c. slightly better than by chance alone
   d. none of the above

10. Research suggests that we tend to smile ____ when we are lying.
    a. more
    b. less
    c. differently
    d. longer

11. Kraut and Poe's (1980) study of Customs inspectors' ability to detect "smugglers" showed that
    a. customs inspectors were no better than lay people
    b. customs inspectors were significantly better than lay people
    c. customs inspectors were significantly worse than lay people
    d. none of the above

12. The accuracy of personality judgments depends on
    a. the criteria of accuracy used
    b. the behaviors observed by the judges
    c. the statistical measure of accuracy used
    d. the specific traits being judged
    e. all of the above

13. Luchins's (1957) study in which subjects read a story about a character named "Jim" found strong evidence for a
    a. recency effect
    b. primacy effect
    c. false consensus effect
    d. nonverbal effect

14. Mock jury experiments suggest that jurors
    a. often treat physically attractive defendants more leniently than unattractive defendants
    b. are not influenced by the defendants' verbal and nonverbal behavior
    c. are more influenced by juror bias than by the actual evidence
    d. both A and C

ANSWERS TO COMPLETION ITEMS

1. Person; object   (62)
2. Power; preference   (68)
3. Charles Darwin   (78-80)
4. body; voice   (87)
5. Causal agents   (62)
6. impressions   (65)
7. Adaptors   (68)
8. eye contact; personal space; touching (68-69)
9. social; intellectual   (78-79)
10. universal   (81-82)

ANSWERS TO MATCHING QUESTIONS

1. e   (63-64)
2. f   (63-64)
3. b   (63-64)
4. c   (71)
5. a   (81)
6. d   (70)

ANSWERS TO MULTIPLE CHOICE QUESTIONS

1. b   (61)
2. c   (63)
3. a   (67)
4. b   (66-67)
5. a   (65-66)
6. d   (75)
7. b   (81)
8. a   (87)
9. c   (86-87)
10. c   (90-91)
11. a   (92)
12. e   (73-78)
13. b   (71-72)
14. a   (70-71)

CHAPTER 4

ATTRIBUTION

CHAPTER OUTLINE

I. <u>Attribution Processes: Internal and External Causes</u>

   A. Our Preference for Internal Explanations

II. <u>Theories of Attribution</u>

   A. Jones and Davis's Theory of Correspondent Inferences
      1. Social desirability
      2. Common and noncommon effects
      3. Hedonic relevance and personalism
   B. Kelley's Cube Model of Attribution
      1. Consistency, consensus, and distinctiveness information
      2. The covariation principle
      3. Internal versus external attributions in Kelley's model
      4. Kelley's model tested
   C. Causal Schemas
      1. The discounting principle
      2. Reward and intrinsic motivation
      3. When discounting fails

III. <u>Attribution Errors and Biases</u>

   A. The Fundamental Attribution Error
   B. The Actor-Observer Effect
      1. Research on the actor-observer effect
      2. Reasons for the actor-observer effect
   C. Salience Effects in Attribution
   D. Motivational Biases in Attribution
      1. Self-serving bias
      2. Self-handicapping strategies

IV. <u>Applying Attribution Theory</u>

    A. Treating Depression
    B. Improving Academic Performance

V. <u>Summary</u>

VI. <u>Glossary</u>

LEARNING OBJECTIVES

After reading and studying Chapter 4, you should be able to answer the following questions.

1. What is the major focus of attribution theories? (97)

2. According to Weiner, what two dimensions underlie our explanations of behavior? (99)

3. Describe the relationship between attribution and our emotional experiences. (100-101)

4. Why do we often prefer internal to external explanations of behavior? (100-102)

5. What do Jones and Davis mean by a "correspondent inference"? What four principles do people use in making a correspondent inference? (103-107)

6. Describe the three kinds of information that, according to Kelley's cube model, are crucial in determining our attributions. (107-109)

7. According to Kelley, which patterns of information are likely to induce us to make internal attributions? (108)

8. What is meant by a causal schema? (111)

9. What effect do rewards have on intrinsic motivations? What is meant by the over-justification effect? (112-113)

10. Under what conditions should you not assume that a person's stated and written opinions reflect his or her actual attitudes? (114-115)

11. Give several examples of the fundamental attribution error. (116-117)

12. Describe the actor-observer effect. Discuss several reasons why it occurs. (117-121)

13. What effect does perceptual salience have on our attributions? (122-123)

14. Give an example of the self-serving bias. According to Miller (1978) what are the two main purposes of self-serving attributions? (124)

15. Describe the self-handicapping strategy. Under what conditions are people more likely to engage in self-handicapping behavior? (125-126)

16. Compare the kinds of attributions that depressed and normal people tend to make in explaining their own behavior.

KEY TERMS TO KNOW

After reading and studying Chapter 4, you should be able to define or understand the following terms.

attribution theory (97)
internal versus external explanations (98)
stable versus unstable causes (98)

COMPLETION ITEMS

Fill in the word(s) to complete each of the following statements. Check your responses against the correct answers at the end of this chapter.

1. _____ theories focus on the thought processes people use to explain their own and others' behavior.

2. All other things being equal, people often prefer _____ explanations of behavior.

3. According to the actor-observer effect, actors tend to attribute their own behavior to _____ causes and tend to overemphasize _____ causes in others.

4. Academic anxiety may be reduced by getting students to attribute their academic failures to _____ causes.

5. _____ occurs when subjects are led to attribute their behavior (often arousal) incorrectly.

6. In order to protect their self-esteem, people sometimes engage in a(n) _____ strategy when they anticipate failure.

7. Causal _____ are simple mental models of causality.

8. The _____ principle holds that we assign less weight to a given cause if another plausible cause is also present.

9. Rewards sometimes undermine _____ motivation, especially when they are _____.

10. Studies by McArthur (1972) of Kelley's cube model suggest that people use _____ information less than _____ or _____ information.

MATCHING TERMS AND CONCEPTS

Write the letter of the term or concept from below that best fits the following phrases or sentences. Check your responses against the correct answers at the end of this chapter.

____ 1. Refers to how behavior varies across situations and time

____ 2. Refers to how a person's behavior compares with other people's behavior

____ 3. Refers to how behavior varies as a function of its target

____ 4. Normative or expected in this situation

____ 5. Preference for internal explanations of behavior

____ 6. We tend to make stronger dispositional attributions when behavior directly affects us.

a. distinctiveness
b. consistency
c. social desirability
d. fundamental attribution error
e. hedonic relevance
f. consensus

MULTIPLE CHOICE QUESTIONS

Circle the one best answer to each question.
Check your responses against the correct answers
at the end of this chapter.

1. According to Fritz Heider, an important part
   of the attribution process is deciding
   whether behavior is explained by _____
   causes.
   a. internal or external
   b. stable or unstable
   c. target-based or category-based
   d. intentional or unintentional

2. According to Jones and Davis's theory of
   correspondent inference, _____ lead(s) to
   stronger inferences about a person's
   disposition.
   a. common effects
   b. noncommon effects
   c. socially desirable behavior
   d. distinctiveness

3. Category-based expectancies and target-based
   expectancies affect our judgments of
   a. noncommon effects
   b. consensus
   c. hedonic relevance
   d. social desirability

4. An example of the _____ is when expected
   rewards reduce intrinsic motivation.
   a. misattribution effect
   b. over-justification effect
   c. self-handicapping strategy
   d. hedonic relevance

5. After finding out how you did on the first exam, you ask several of your classmates how they did. According to Kelley's cube model, you are seeking _____ information.
   a. consistency   c. distinctiveness
   b. consensus   d. discounting

6. In Weiner's two-dimensional model of attribution, which of the following is the best example of internal, unstable causal attribution?
   a. good or bad luck
   b. ability or intelligence
   c. effort
   d. degree of task difficulty

7. The tendency to overemphasize internal explanations and underemphasize external causes has been called the
   a. actor-observer effect
   b. salience effect
   c. self-handicapping strategy
   d. fundamental attribution error

8. In attribution theory, which of the following terms is used as an internal explanation of behavior?
   a. situational cause
   b. environmental cause
   c. dispositional cause
   d. none of the above

9. According to research by Nisbett and his colleagues (1973), we are less likely to make the fundamental attribution error when explaining
   a. the behavior of someone famous like Walter Cronkite
   b. our own behavior
   c. the behavior of our parents
   d. the behavior of our best friend

10. Depressed people tend to attribute their failures to _____ factors and their successes to _____ factors.
    a. internal; external
    b. consistency; inconsistent
    c. common; noncommon
    d. external; internal

11. Kelley's cube model of attribution is based on
    a. the covariation principle
    b. extrinsic motivation
    c. the hedonic relevance principle
    d. the personalism principle

12. The classic experiment by Schachter and Singer demonstrated that subjects experienced the strongest emotions when they received injections of _____ and were _____ of its side effects.
    a. saline; informed
    b. saline; misinformed
    c. epinephrine; informed
    d. epinephrine; misinformed

ANSWERS TO COMPLETION ITEMS

1. Attribution (97)
2. internal (100)
3. external or situational; internal or dispositional (117)
4. external (129)
5. Misattribution (101)
6. self-handicapping (125)
7. schemas (111)
8. discounting (111)
9. intrinsic; expected (112-113)
10. consensus; consistency; distinctiveness (110-111)

ANSWERS TO MATCHING QUESTIONS

1. b (107)
2. f (107)
3. a (107)
4. c (104)
5. d (116)
6. e (106)

ANSWERS TO MULTIPLE CHOICE QUESTIONS

 1. a (98)
 2. b (106)
 3. d (105)
 4. b (112-113)
 5. b (107)
 6. c (99)
 7. d (116)
 8. c (98)
 9. b (117, 120-121)
10. a (128)
11. a (107)
12. d (100-101)

CHAPTER 5

SOCIAL COGNITION

CHAPTER OUTLINE

I. <u>Putting Information Together: Impression Formation</u>

    A. Asch's Gestalt Model
    B. Anderson's Weighted Averaging Model

II. <u>Schemas and Social Perception</u>

    A. The Nature of Schemas
    B. Kinds of Schemas in Social Cognition
    C. Effects of Schemas on Social Cognition
        1. Schemas can influence perception
        2. Schemas can influence memory
        3. Schemas can influence social inference
        4. Schemas can influence behavior
        5. Priming effects
    D. The Persistence of Schemas
    E. Illusory Correlations in Social Perception

III. <u>Social Inference and Decision Making</u>

    A. The Effects of Sampling Errors on Inferences
    B. The Underutilization of Baserate Information
    C. Heuristics -- Shortcuts to Social Inference
        1. The availability heuristic
        2. The representativeness heuristic
    D. Framing Effects in Decision Making

IV. <u>Social Cognition: A Final Thought</u>

V. <u>Summary</u>

VI. <u>Glossary</u>

LEARNING OBJECTIVES

After reading and studying Chapter 5, you should be able to answer the following questions.

1. What is social cognition? What are the main topics in social cognition? (133-134)

2. What is impression formation? (135)

3. Describe Asch's Gestalt model of impression formation. What does he mean by a "central trait"? (135-137)

4. According to Anderson's weighted averaging model, how do people combine trait information about others? What kind of information tends to be weighted more heavily? (137-139)

5. What are schemas? List and briefly describe the four main kinds of schemas. (140-142)

6. Summarize the results of the study by Duncan (1976) where students watched a videotape in which either a black student shoved a white student or vice versa. (144-146)

7. Describe the effect of schemas on memory. (145-148)

8. Describe how we evaluate in-groups and out-groups differently. What were the results of Linville and Jones's (1980) study of white and black law school applicants? (148-150)

9. How can schemas influence behavior? (151-152)

10. Describe the effects of priming. (152-153)

11. What is the perseverance effect? (154)

12. What is meant by illusory correlations in
    social perception? (155-156)

13. Describe several common errors people make in
    social inference and decision making.
    (157-166)

14. What is a heuristic? Describe the available
    and representativeness heuristics. (160-163)

15. What is the framing effect? (163-166)

KEY TERMS TO KNOW

After reading and studying Chapter 5, you should
be able to define or understand the following
terms.

social cognition (133)
impression formation (134)
schemas (134)
Asch's Gestalt Model (135-137)
central traits (136)
Anderson's weighted averaging model (137-139)
primacy effect (138)
features (141)
prototypes (142)
person, self-, role-, and event schemas (142)
memory-based inferences (150)
self-fulfilling prophecy (151)
priming effects (152)
perseverance effect (154)
illusory correlations (155-157)
sampling errors (157-159)
baserate information (160)
linear and nonlinear decison rules (159)
availability heuristic (161)
representativeness heuristic (162)
dilution effect (163)

COMPLETION ITEMS

Fill in the word(s) to complete each of the
following statements. Check your responses
against the correct answers at the end of this
chapter.

1. _____ is the study of how people
   process information about other people.

2. Research indicates that it is easier for us
   to remember information that is _____
   with our schemas.

3. Schemas are often _____ to change.

4. "The whole is greater than the sum of its
   parts" is descriptive of _____ theory.

5. Anderson's weighted averaging model considers
   the "_____" trait to be a particularly
   heavily weighted piece of information.

6. The _____ effect occurs when social
   judgments are influenced by the way a
   question is worded or posed.

7. _____ are shortcut cognitive processes
   that give quick estimates and answers.

8. The _____ effect occurs when a schema that
   has been recently used is more readily
   available for subsequent use.

9. People may falsely see _____ correlations
   between variables based on their preconceived
   notions.

MATCHING TERMS AND CONCEPTS

Write the letter of the term or concept from below that best fits the following phrases or sentences. Check your responses against the correct answers at the end of this chapter.

____ 1. Mental category that describes typical or specific individuals

____ 2. Mental categories describing broad social groups or roles

____ 3. Refers to ways in which we classify and describe ourselves

____ 4. Our mental categorization of social events like "going to class"

____ 5. Ideal or perfect examples of a category

____ 6. How we organize information about other people into meaningful wholes

____ 7. The study of how people process information about other people

____ 8. The process by which people's expectations become reality

a. prototypes
b. role-schemas
c. person schema
d. self-schemas
e. event schemas
f. self-fulfilling prophecy
g. impression formation
h. social cognition

MULTIPLE CHOICE QUESTIONS

Circle the one best answer to each question.
Check your responses against the correct answers
at the end of this chapter.

1. Research indicates that in forming
   impressions of likability, subjects often
   weigh _____ information more heavily than
   _____ information.
   a. positive; negative
   b. negative; positive
   c. moderate; extreme
   d. positive; extreme

2. In impression formation, which traits did
   Asch consider to be "central" traits?
   a. happy and sad
   b. wise and foolish
   c. warm and cold
   d. polite and blunt

3. Linville and Jones's (1980) study of white
   and black law school applicants found that
   a. blacks were all evaluated higher
   b. whites were all evaluated higher
   c. blacks with weak credentials were rated
      higher
   d. we evaluate members of in-groups and
      out-groups differently

4. The _____ effect occurs when people
   maintain beliefs that have been disconfirmed.
   a. perseverance   c. priming
   b. dilution   d. framing

5. Schemas can affect
   a. our perception of social information
   b. our memory for social information
   c. social behavior
   d. all of the above

6. Duncan's (1976) study, in which students watched a videotape where one student shoves another student, showed that the students' perception of the shove as being violent
   a. depended on the sex of the student being shoved
   b. depended on the race of the student doing the shoving
   c. depended on the age of the students
   d. all of the above

7. A schema that has been recently used is more readily available for subsequent use. This is usually called the _____ effect.
   a. priming   c. primacy
   b. dilution   d. perseverance

8. _____ theory suggests that a given positive event is perceived somewhat differently than an equivalent negative event.
   a. Algebraic
   b. Weight averaging
   c. Prospect
   d. Gestalt

9. The _____ heuristic refers to estimating the frequency of an event according to the ease with which we can recall relevant instances.
   a. representative   c. baserate
   b. availability   d. primacy

10. Allport and Postman's (1947/1965) study of rumor transmission demonstrated how
    a. memory is better for inconsistent information
    b. schemas can influence our perceptions of events
    c. the priming effect takes place
    d. social perception is affected by illusory correlations

ANSWERS TO COMPLETION ITEMS

1. Social cognition (133)
2. consistent (145)
3. resistant (154)
4. Gestalt (136)
5. central (138)
6. framing (163)
7. Heuristics (161)
8. priming (152)
9. illusory (155)

ANSWERS TO MATCHING QUESTIONS

1. c (142)
2. b (142)
3. d (142)
4. e (142)
5. a (142)
6. g (134)
7. h (133)
8. f (151)

ANSWERS TO MULTIPLE CHOICE QUESTIONS

1. b (137-139)
2. c (135-137)
3. d (148-150)
4. a (154)
5. d (142)
6. b (144-146)
7. a (152)
8. c (165)
9. b (161-162)
10. b (143)

CHAPTER 6

PERSONALITY AND THE SELF

CHAPTER OUTLINE

I. <u>Personality and Social Behavior</u>

   A. Trait Theories: Personality as Stable
      Internal Dispositions
      1. The measurement of personality traits
   B. Social Learning Theories: Personality as
      Learned Behavior
   C. Research on Personality Theories
      1. Research on the assumptions of trait
         theories
      2. The interaction between traits and
         situations
      3. Moderator variables
      4. Self-monitoring

II. <u>The Self</u>

   A. Classic Views of the Self
      1. The self and social feedback
      2. The "I" versus the "me"
      3. Development of the self
   B. Self-Knowledge -- Research on the "Me"
      1. The self as a schema
      2. Schematic people as experts on the self
      3. The complexity of the self-schema
      4. The self's resistance to change
      5. Self-verification versus self-
         enhancement
   C. Self-Awareness Theory
      1. The consequences of self-directed
         attention
      2. Self-awareness and internal standards
      3. A control model of self
      4. Self-discrepancy

        D. Public and Private Selves
            1. Impression management: The self as an
               actor
        E. The Self and Mental Health
            1. Self-awareness and depression
            2. Breaking the cycle of depression
            3. Cognitive complexity and depression

III. Summary

IV. Glossary

LEARNING OBJECTIVES

After reading and studying Chapter 6, you should
be able to answer the following questions.

1. How do psychologists define the term
   personality? (173)

2. What kinds of explanations are emphasized by
   trait theories and social learning theories?
   (175-177)

3. What are the five basic trait dimensions of
   personality that have been repeatedly found
   in research? (175)

4. Describe several important properties of a
   good personality test? (176)

5. How do trait and social learning theories
   differ in their prediction of individual
   behavior? (177-181)

6. Define and give several examples of a
   moderator variable. (179)

7. Compare "strong" versus "weak" situations in
   determining the effects traits have on
   behavior. (182-183)

8. According to Snyder, how do the concepts of self differ for low and high self-monitors? (184)

9. Compare and contrast low and high self-monitors' behavioral tendencies in everyday life. (183-186)

10. Under what conditions do traits best predict behavior? (189)

11. What is implied by the concept of "self"? Do animals other than human beings have a concept of self? (189-190)

12. What kinds of explanations of behavior are emphasized in concepts of the "self"? (191-193)

13. How do self-schemas influence how we process information about ourselves and others? (194-201)

14. Describe several ways in which we avoid self-awareness after failure. (202-203)

15. Describe several differences between the control model of self and a thermostat control. (205)

16. Describe Goffman's view of the public self. (207-208)

17. Give several examples of how people "bask in the reflected glory." Why do people engage in this kind of behavior? (209)

18. Discuss how self-awareness can contribute to depression. (210-211)

KEY TERMS TO KNOW

After reading and studying Chapter 6, you should be able to define or understand the following terms.

personality (173)
mediating variables (173)
trait theories (175)
test-retest reliability (176)
internal reliability (176)
predictive validity (176)
construct validity (176)
discriminant validity (176)
social learning theories (176)
moderator variable (179)
"weak" versus "strong" situations (182)
precipitating situations (182)
self-monitoring (183)
principled and pragmatic concepts of self (184)
"self" (190)
looking glass self (191)
"the generalized other" (191)
"I" versus "me" (191)
self-schema (194)
self-reference effect (198)
self-verification (199)
self-enhancement (200)
self-awareness theory (201)
control model of self (203)
self-discrepancy (206)
impression management (208)
the public self (208)
basking in the reflected glory (209)
reactive depression (211)
cognitive complexity (213)

COMPLETION ITEMS

Fill in the word(s) to complete each of the following statements. Check your responses against the correct answers at the end of this chapter.

1. _____ refers to the consistent, stable, and distinctive traits and behaviors that characterize individuals.

2. _____ theories assume that people possess consistent internal dispositions that have a general influence on behavior.

3. People who are _____ on self-complexity are more likely to become depressed after receiving negative information about themselves.

4. Early personality research suggested that behavior is often _____ across settings.

5. People in "_____" situations behave more as the situation dictates, while people in "_____" situations behave in a manner more consistent with their traits.

6. People often remember information that is related to _____ better than they remember other kinds of information.

7. A test has _____ reliability when test scores show consistent results when taken at two different times by the same people.

8. Research by Duval and Wicklund suggests that we avoid self-awareness after_____.

9. _____ comprise the organized knowledge people possess about themselves.

10. The _____ model of self proposes that the self acts as a control system that attempts to match behavior to internal standards when the self is in a state of self-directed attention.

11. Self-_____ refers to regulating one's behavior to fit social demands or situational norms.

MATCHING TERMS AND CONCEPTS

Write the letter of the term or concept from below that best fits the following phrases or sentences. Check your responses against the correct answers at the end of this chapter.

____ 1. A personality test predicts relevant criteria.

____ 2. A personality test correlates with theoretically related variables.

____ 3. A variable that determines the effect one variable has on another variable

____ 4. Publicly associating ourselves with successful people

____ 5. Means an actor's mask

____ 6. The vison of self that is reflected to us from communication with other people

a. looking glass self
b. persona
c. construct validity
d. moderator
e. basking in the reflected glory
f. predictive validity

MULTIPLE CHOICE QUESTIONS

Circle the one best answer to each question.
Check your responses against the correct answers
at the end of this chapter.

1. According to social learning theories, the
   personality resides in each persons' unique
   a. pattern of behavior and learning history
   b. traits
   c. internal dispositions
   d. heredity and physiology

2. The central issue(s) of personality research
   are
   a. the internal causes of behavior
   b. individual differences
   c. the consistency of behavior
   d. all of the above

3. Traits best predict behaviors that are _____
   the trait.
   a. inconsistent with
   b. prototypical of
   c. the opposite of
   d. all of the above

4. High self-monitor individuals have a _____
   concept of self.
   a. principled
   b. pragmatic
   c. trait
   d. inner

5. Studies indicate that depressed people have
   _____ self-awareness in general compared to
   nondepressed people.
   a. higher
   b. lower
   c. little
   d. a positive

6. Under which condition would you be least
   likely to be self-aware?
   a. when you look into a mirror
   b. when taking an oral exam
   c. when being videotaped for a TV interview
   d. when watching your favorite TV program

7. People engage in self-verification behavior
   by
   a. selectively seeking feedback that confirms
      their self-concept
   b. selectively remembering feedback that
      confirms their self-concept
   c. actively trying to prove to others the
      truth of their self-concept
   d. all of the above

8. People who are high on private self-
   consciousness behave in ways that are
   more _____ with their inner traits,
   attitudes and values.
   a. inconsistent
   b. consistent
   c. out of touch
   d. none of the above

9. Compared to low self-monitors, high
   self-monitors
   a. change their behavior to fit the situation
   b. behave in a way that is more consistent
      with their inner traits
   c. tend to be more committed to one partner
      in a relationship
   d. are attracted to other people on the basis
      of external appearances

10. _____ suggests that life is a theatrical
    stage with acting roles that we each play.
    a. The control model
    b. Impression management
    c. The self-reference effect
    d. The self-discrepancy model

ANSWERS TO COMPLETION ITEMS

  1. Personality (173)
  2. Trait (175)
  3. low (213)
  4. inconsistent (179)
  5. strong; weak (182-183)
  6. the self (197)
  7. test-retest (176)
  8. failure (201-202)
  9. Self-schemas (194-195)
10. control (204-205)
11. monitoring (183-184)

ANSWERS TO MATCHING QUESTIONS

  1. f (176)
  2. c (176)
  3. d (180)
  4. e (209)
  5. b (172)
  6. a (191)

ANSWERS TO MULTIPLE CHOICE QUESTIONS

  1. a (177)
  2. d (175)
  3. b (178)
  4. b (184)
  5. a (211-212)
  6. d (202)
  7. d (200)
  8. b (204)
  9. a (183-188)
10. b (208)

CHAPTER 7

ATTITUDES AND BELIEFS

CHAPTER OUTLINE

I. <u>What Are Attitudes?</u>

    A. Characteristics of Attitudes
    B. A Functional Approach to Attitudes
    C. Attitude Measurement
       1. Thurstone scales
       2. Likert scales
       3. Semantic differential scales
       4. The validity of attitude scales
       5. Behavioral measures of attitude

II. <u>Attitude Formation</u>

    A. Learning Theories of Attitude Formation
       1. Classical conditioning
       2. Operant conditioning
       3. Modeling and observational learning
       4. Implications of learning theories
    B. Personality and Attitude Formation
    C. Logical Inference Theories
       1. Attitude and belief systems
       2. Mathematical models of consistency
    D. Self-Perception Theory

III. <u>Attitudes and Behavior</u>

    A. Difficulties in Predicting Behavior from Attitudes
       1. The effects of other influential variables
       2. Improper measures of attitudes
       3. Improper measures of behavior
    B. Fishbein and Ajzen's Theory of Reasoned Action

LEARNING OBJECTIVES

After reading and studying Chapter 7, you should be able to answer the following questions.

1. How do psychologists define an attitude? How are attitudes different from beliefs? (221)

2. According to Katz (1960), what are the four basic functions of attitudes? (222)

3. Describe the three major scaling methods for measuring attitudes. Briefly describe the important steps in developing an attitude scale. (223-229)

4. Describe several behavioral measures that have been used to infer attitudes. (229)

5. Describe how attitudes are learned through the processes of classical conditioning, operant conditioning, and modeling. (230-236)

6. Explain how personality may play a role in attitude formation. (237)

7. How do the logical inference theories suggest that attitudes are developed? (238-239)

8. How does self-perception theory propose that attitudes are formed? (240-241)

9. Describe the study by LaPiere (1934). What did this study suggest about the relationship between attitudes and behavior? (243-244)

10. Describe three major reasons why attitudes don't necessarily strongly predict behavior. (244-246)

11. Explain Fishbein and Ajzen's theory of reasoned action. What is the relationship between attitudes, subjective norms, behavioral intentions, and behavior? (247-251)

12. When do attitudes best predict behavior? (247-251)

KEY TERMS TO KNOW

After reading and studying Chapter 7, you should be able to define or understand the following terms.

attitudes (221)
instrumental function (222)
ego-defense function (222)
knowledge function (222)
value-expressive function (222)
attitude scales (223-229)
Thurstone scales (223)
Likert scales (224-226)
semantic differential scales (226)
bogus pipeline method (226)
Galvanic Skin Response (229)
classical conditioning (230)
unconditioned stimulus (230)
unconditioned response (230)

COMPLETION ITEMS

Fill in the word(s) to complete each of the
following statements. Check your responses
against the correct answers at the end of this
chapter.

1. An attitude is a(n) _____ evaluative
   response, directed at specific objects, that
   is relatively _____ and influences
   _____ in a general motivating way.

2. Attitudes may serve _____,
   _____, _____, and
   _____ functions.

3. Thurstone scales, Likert scales and semantic
   differential ratings are three types of
   _____ measurement techniques.

4. Beliefs that are not based on other beliefs
   are called _____ beliefs.

5. Learning theory suggests that we form attitudes through _____ conditioning, _____ conditioning, and through _____ and observation.

6. Self-_____ theory suggests that people examine their behavior to infer their attitudes.

7. Subjective norms refers to beliefs about how significant _____ wish us to behave.

8. _____ occurs in classical conditioning when people show a conditioned response not only to a specific stimulus but to other similar stimuli.

9. Operant conditioning occurs when _____ and _____ influence voluntary behaviors.

MATCHING TERMS AND CONCEPTS

Write the letter of the term or concept from below that best fits the following phrases or sentences. Check your responses against the correct answers at the end of this chapter.

____ 1. The most commonly used attitude scaling technique

____ 2. A technique to induce subjects to answer attitude questionnaires more honestly

____ 3. A conditioned response not only to a specific stimulus but also to related words and stimuli

____ 4. The kind of learning that takes place when voluntary responses are rewarded

____ 5. Cognitive information that need not have an emotional component

____ 6. The kind of learning that occurs when people observe another's behavior or attitude and imitate it

____ 7. Beliefs about how significant others wish us to behave

____ 8. Scales of evaluative meaning (e.g., good-bad) used to measure attitudes

a. operant conditioning
b. belief
c. Likert scaling
d. semantic differential scales
e. bogus pipeline
f. subjective norms
g. attitudes
h. semantic generalization
i. modeling

MULTIPLE CHOICE QUESTIONS

Circle the one best answer to each question. Check your responses against the correct answers at the end of this chapter.

1. Attitudes are
   a. a learned evaluative response
   b. directed at some object or target
   c. relatively enduring
   d. all of the above

2. A study by Porier and Lott (1967) indicated that subjects who were more prejudiced against blacks tended to show _____ when touched by a black research assistant.
   a. greater Galvanic Skin Response
   b. less Galvanic Skin Response
   c. less eye contact
   d. none of the above

3. A father praises a child every time the child expresses an attitude similar to his own. The child is forming attitudes through
   a. classical conditioning
   b. operant conditioning
   c. self-perception learning
   d. diffusion

4. If you adopt an attitude because it helps to structure complex information about the world, it is serving
   a. an ego-defense function
   b. a knowledge function
   c. a value-expressive function
   d. an instrumental function

5. According to Fishbein and Ajzen's theory of reasoned action, attitudes and subjective norms combine to influence _____, which ultimately determine your behavior.
   a. self-perceptions   c. values
   b. behavioral intentions   d. beliefs

6. Attitude best predicts behavior when
   a. measuring classes of behavior
   b. the time interval between measuring the attitude and behavior is brief
   c. the attitudes and behaviors correspond in their level of generality or specificity
   d. all of the above

7. The classic study by LaPiere (1934) of hotel and restaurant employees' reactions to a Chinese couple suggested that
   a. attitudes and behavior show little relationship
   b. attitudes and behavior are related
   c. discrimination was more prevalent in hotels than restaurants
   d. both b and c

8. The most commonly used type(s) of attitude measurement
   a. are physiological measures
   b. is the bogus pipeline
   c. are self-report questionnaires
   d. are behavioral measures

9. According to reasoned action theory, if your goal is to predict behavior, it is best
   a. to measure personality traits
   b. to measure attitudes toward objects
   c. to measure attitude toward the behavior
   d. to wait a long time between measurements of attitude and behavior

10. Research suggests that self-perception processes are most likely to occur when
    a. attitudes are weak or ambiguous
    b. attitudes are inferred from attitudes
    c. attitudes are learned through rewards
    d. all of the above

11. The logical inference theories suggest that attitudes are
    a. logically inferred from behavior
    b. logically inferred from other beliefs and attitudes
    c. logically inferred from our personality
    d. dependent on logical learning principles

12. An attitude is best defined as a learned
    _____ response directed at specific objects.
    a. emotional   c. behavioral
    b. evaluative   d. none of the above

ANSWERS TO COMPLETION ITEMS

1. learned; enduring; behavior (221)
2. instrumental; ego-defense; knowledge;
   value-expressive (222-223)
3. attitude (223-229)
4. primitive (238)
5. classical; operant; modeling (230)
6. perception (240-241)
7. others (247)
8. Generalization (232)
9. rewards; punishments (234)

ANSWERS TO MATCHING QUESTIONS

1. c (224-226)   5. b (238)
2. e (226)   6. i (236)
3. h (232)   7. f (247)
4. a (234)   8. d (226)

ANSWERS TO MULTIPLE CHOICE QUESTIONS

1. d (221)   7. a (243)
2. a (229)   8. c (229)
3. b (234)   9. c (248)
4. b (222-223)   10. a (240-242)
5. b (247)   11. b (237-239)
6. d (246-251)   12. b (221)

CHAPTER 8

PERSUASION AND ATTITUDE CHANGE

CHAPTER OUTLINE

I. <u>A Communication Model of Persuasion:
   The Yale Research</u>

   A. Communicator Variables
   B. Message Variables
      1. Fear appeals
      2. One-sided vs. two-sided messages
      3. Message repetition
   C. Channel Variables
   D. Target or Audience Variables
   E. Interactions Among Persuasion Variables

II. <u>Dissonance Theory and Research</u>

   A. Festinger's Theory of Cognitive Dissonance
   B. The Festinger and Carlsmith (1959) Study
   C. The Psychology of Insufficient
      Justification
   D. Variations on a Dissonance Theme
      1. Insufficient threat: The "forbidden
         toy" study
      2. Severity of initiation
      3. Derogation of the victim
   E. Qualifications on Dissonance Theory
      1. Free choice
      2. Commitment and irrevocability
      3. Consequences of behavior
   F. Self-Perception Theory: An Alternate
      Explanation
   G. Evaluating Dissonance Theory and
      Self-Perception Theory

III. <u>Cognitive Responses and Attitude Change</u>

   A. Forewarning Effects

B. Attitudes as Schemas

IV. The Elaboration Likelihood Model of Persuasion

V. Summary

VI. Glossary

LEARNING OBJECTIVES

After reading and studying Chapter 8, you should be able to answer the following questions.

1. List and briefly describe the four variables in the communication model of persuasion. (257-258)

2. What are the immediate and long-term effects of communicators' credibility on persuasion? (258-260)

3. List several variables that make a message persuasive. (261-264)

4. Explain under what conditions fear appeals are effective. (261)

5. What does research suggest about the effectiveness of one-sided versus two-sided messages? Which produces greater resistance to counterpropaganda? (262)

6. Describe the mere exposure effect. (262-263)

7. Under what conditions (e.g., communicator likability) are the various channels of communication more effective? (264-266)

8. How does the "need for cognition" affect the audience's response to a persuasion message? (267-268)

9. Describe Festinger's theory of cognitive dissonance. How does cognitive dissonance theory explain attitude change? (272-274)

10. Briefly describe the classic study by Festinger and Carlsmith (1959). How were the results explained by dissonance theory? (274-275)

11. When does counterattitudinal behavior lead to disssonance and attitude change? What qualifying conditions affect the impact of dissonance on attitude change? (275-283)

12. Describe how dissonance theory applies to research on insufficient threat, severity of initiation, and derogation of the victim. (278-280)

13. How does self-perception theory explain the results of the insufficient justification studies? (283-286)

14. When does research suggest that self-perception processes and dissonance are more likely to occur? (286-288)

15. What does research suggest about the effect of forewarning people in terms of resistance to persuasion? (289)

16. Describe the effects of rhetorical questions on persuasion. (289)

17. What are the three principal approaches to understanding attitude change? (292)

18. Summarize the elaboration likelihood model of persuasion. Compare and contrast peripheral and central routes to persuasion. (293-296)

KEY TERMS TO KNOW

After reading and studying Chapter 8, you should be able to define or understand the following terms.

communication model of persuasion (257-258)
communicator variables (258-260)
credibility (258)
sleeper effect (259)
fear appeals (261)
message variables (261)
one-sided versus two-sided messages (262)
mere exposure effect (262)
channel variables (264-267)
audience variables (266-269)
need for cognition (267)
cognitive dissonance theory (269-273)
counterattitudinal behavior (275)
insufficient justification (275)
insufficient threat (278)
severity of initiation (279)
irrevocable choice (283)
self-perception theory (283-289)
cognitive response theory (289)
forewarning effects (289)
rhetorical questions (289)
inoculation effect (290-291)
elaboration likelihood model (293)
central and peripheral routes (293)

COMPLETION ITEMS

Fill in the word(s) to complete each of the following statements. Check your responses against the correct answers at the end of this chapter.

1. The Yale research is based on a(n) _____ and learning model of persuasion.

2. The _____ effect occurs when a message from a low-credibility communicator is more persuasive after a time delay.

3. _____-sided messages are more persuasive to people who already disagree with the message.

4. Festinger (1957) proposed that peole experience cognitive _____ when they hold inconsistent beliefs.

5. _____-to-_____ persuasion often has more impact than media persuasion.

6. Studies suggest that _____ people ahead of time that they will be the target of a persuasion attempt makes them more resistant to persuasion.

7. According to the elaboration likelihood model of persuasion, there are two routes to persuasion called the _____ route and _____ route.

8. Credibility, status, and attractiveness are examples of _____ variables in the communication model of persuasion.

9. Aronson and Mills (1959) demonstrated that the _____ of initiation increases our liking for the group.

MATCHING TERMS AND CONCEPTS

Write the letter of the term or concept from below that best fits the following phrases or sentences. Check your responses against the correct answers at the end of this chapter.

___ 1. The tendency to like stimuli the more frequently we are exposed to them

___ 2. The discomfort arising from inconsistent beliefs

___ 3. Internal arguments for or against a persuasive message

___ 4. Medium through which a persuasive message is delivered

___ 5. The tendency to think about arguments in persuasive messages

a. channel
b. cognitive responses
c. mere exposure effect
d. need for cognition
e. dissonance
f. source variables

MULTIPLE CHOICE QUESTIONS

Circle the one best answer to each question. Check your responses against the correct answers at the end of this chapter.

1. Which of the following is <u>not</u> one of the four major variables in the communication model of persuasion?
   a. communicator   c. message
   b. channel   d. cognitive

2. Counterattitudinal behavior is more likely to lead to dissonance when the behavior is
   a. freely chosen
   b. firmly committed
   c. irrevocable
   d. all of the above

3. The _____ route to persuasion is being used when attitude change occurs without careful thought about the issues.
   a. central   c. peripheral
   b. message   d. primary

4. The findings from Festinger and Carlsmith's (1959) study on insufficient justification were originally explained by
   a. cognitive dissonance theory
   b. self-perception theory
   c. the communication model of attitude change
   d. the elaboration likelihood model

5. The _____ effect involves presenting people with weak arguments against a position that are refuted to enable them to later resist strong persuasive messages.
   a. mere exposure   c. inoculation
   b. fear appeal   d. sleeper

6. _____ messages seem to be less affected by the characteristics of the source.
   a. Written
   b. Audio
   c. Videotaped
   d. Face-to-face

7. The _____ model suggests that there are two routes (central and peripheral) to persusaion.
   a. cognitive dissonance
   b. Yale communication and learning
   c. elaboration likelihood
   d. self-perception

8. Fazio, Zanna, and Cooper (1977) suggest that dissonance theory best applies to attitude-_____ behavior and self-perception theory more than to attitude-_____ behavior.
   a. discrepant; congruent
   b. congruent; related
   c. source; channel
   d. congruent; discrepant

9. Which of the following procedures is likely to produce resistance to attitude change?
   a. forewarning
   b. inoculation
   c. sleeper effect
   d. credibility
   e. both a and b

10. The need for cognition is an example of a _____ variable.
    a. source
    b. channel
    c. message
    d. target

11. Fear appeals are effective when
    a. the message arouses a lot of fear
    b. there are clear recommendations on how to avoid the feared outcome
    c. the target believes the fearful outcome are likely to occur
    d. all of the above

12. The impact of rhetorical questions on attitude change gives support to
    a. cognitive dissonance theory
    b. cognitive response theory
    c. self-perception theory
    d. none of the above

ANSWERS TO COMPLETION ITEMS

1. communication (258)
2. sleeper (259-260)
3. Two (262)
4. dissonance (272)
5. Face; face (264)
6. forewarning or warning (289)
7. central; peripheral (293)
8. source (258)
9. severity (279)

ANSWERS TO MATCHING QUESTIONS

1. c (262)
2. e (272)
3. b (289)
4. a (264)
5. d (267)

ANSWERS TO MULTIPLE CHOICE QUESTIONS

 1. d (258)
 2. d (280)
 3. c (293)
 4. a (274-275)
 5. c (290-291)
 6. a (264)
 7. c (293)
 8. a (288)
 9. e (289-291)
10. d (266)
11. d (261)
12. b (289)

CHAPTER 9

PREJUDICE

CHAPTER OUTLINE

I. <u>What Is Prejudice</u>?

    A. Analyzing Prejudice
        1. Historical analysis
        2. Sociocultural factors
        3. The social situation
        4. Personality and prejudice
        5. The phenomenology of prejudice
        6. The stimulus object

II. <u>Stereotypes</u>

    A. Measuring Stereotypes
        1. Stereotypes as probabilistic beliefs
        2. The diagnostic ratio approach
    B. The Formation of Stereotypes
        1. Sampling errors and stereotypes
        2. Memory limitations and stereotypes
        3. Stereotypes as illusory correlations
    C. Consequences of Stereotypes
        1. Stereotypes and schematic processing
        2. Racial slurs and schematic processing
        3. The self-perpetuating nature of
           stereotypes

III. <u>Social Causes of Prejudice</u>

    A. The Authoritarian Personality
        1. Criticisms of the research
    B. Social Ideologies and Prejudice
        1. Political beliefs and prejudice
        2. Religious beliefs and prejudice
    C. Social Groups and Prejudice
        1. Research on the minimal group
        2. Social identity theory

3. In-group favoritism and self-esteem
4. Out-group derogation and self-esteem
D. Intergroup Competition and Prejudice
   1. Creating prejudice: The Red Devils and the Bull Dogs
   2. Defusing intergroup hostility: The Robber's Cave study

IV. <u>Reducing Prejudice: The Intergroup Contact Hypothesis</u>

A. Contact Between Groups in School
B. The Effect of Contact on Intergroup Attitudes
C. Residential Contact
D. Vicarious Contact Through the Mass Media

V. <u>Summary</u>

VI. <u>Glossary</u>

LEARNING OBJECTIVES

After reading and studying Chapter 9, you should be able to answer the following questions.

1. What is prejudice and how is it defined? What is the difference between prejudice and discrimination? (302-303)

2. List and briefly describe Allport's six different levels that can be used to analyze prejudice. (303-306)

3. What is the nature of stereotypes and prejudicial beliefs? (307)

4. Describe several methods that have been developed to measure stereotypes. How are diagnostic ratios used to measure stereotypes? (307-309)

5. Summarize some of the errors and differences in our social perception of in-groups versus out-groups. (310-311)

6. List and briefly describe several cognitive processes that contribute to the development of stereotypes. (310-315)

7. What are illusory correlations? How are they related to stereotypes? (314-315)

8. Describe some of the consequences of stereotypes in terms of how we process information about members of other groups, how we treat them, and how they respond to us. (316-318)

9. Give an overall description of a high authoritarian in terms of upbringing, behavior, and beliefs. What criticisms have been made of the authoritarian personality research? (319-322)

10. Summarize some of the research findings on the relationship between prejudice and political and religous beliefs. (322-325)

11. What is a stigma? Why are people who have stigmas treated so badly in our society? (324)

12. What is the effect of being in a minimal group? How does Tajfel's theory of social identity explain the in-group favoritism? (325-327)

13. Describe Sherif's Robber's Cave studies. What does this research suggest about the relationship between intergroup competition and prejudice? (328-331)

14. Based on the intergroup contact hypothesis, what kinds of contact are necessary in order to reduce prejudice between groups? (331-339)

15. Describe some of the reasons for the "mixed" effects of school integration on prejudice and achievement. (332-334)

16. According to Wilder (1984), when does interaction with a member of an out-group change our attitude toward the group? (334-336)

17. What is the relationship between prejudice and residental segregation? Is housing integration effective in reducing prejudice and stereotypes? (337-339)

18. Describe the influence of the mass media on both increasing and decreasing prejudice. (338-339)

KEY TERMS TO KNOW

After reading and studying Chapter 9, you should be able to define or understand the following terms.

prejudice (302)
discrimination (303)
segregation (303)
authoritarian personality (319-321)
stereotype (307)
stimulus object (306)
earned reputation theory (306)
diagnostic ratio (308-310)
ethnocentrism (310)
illusion of homogeneity (310-311)
sampling errors (311-312)
illusory correlations (314-315)

schematic processing (316)
self-perpetuating (318)
F scale (319)
Anti-Semitism scale (320)
Ethnocentrism scale (320)
defense mechanisms (321)
dogmatism (322)
symbolic racism (323)
stigma (324)
just world hypothesis (324)
minimal group (325-326)
theory of social identity (326-327)
superordinate goal (329)
intergroup contact hypothesis (331)
equal status contact (331)

COMPLETION ITEMS

Fill in the word(s) to complete each of the
following statements. Check your responses
against the correct answers at the end of this
chapter.

1. _____ refers to overt acts that
   treat members of certain groups unfairly.

2. The _____ approach to prejudice
   focuses on concepts such as urbanization,
   class mobility, and density.

3. Research supports the hypothesis that
   stereotypes about _____ -groups are often
   more negative than those about ____-groups.

4. The research on the _____
   personality suggests that prejudice is
   influenced by child-rearing practices and
   personality dynamics.

5. According to the _____ _____ hypothesis,
   people get their "just deserts."

6. Sherif's summer camp studies showed that intergroup _____ leads to prejudice.

7. Prejudice may be reduced by equal status _____ between majority and minority groups in pursuit of common goals.

8. _____ are overgeneralized and often inaccurate beliefs we hold about groups and group members.

9. _____ group research shows that when people are arbitrarily divided into groups, they show bias in favor of their in-group.

10. Research suggests that political _____ is correlated with prejudice in the U.S.

MATCHING TERMS AND CONCEPTS

Write the letter of the term or concept from below that best fits the following phrases or sentences. Check your responses against the correct answers at the end of this chapter.

____ 1. Physical separation from out-group members

____ 2. The belief that one's own group is superior to other groups

____ 3. Psychological devices used to express feelings in disguised ways

____ 4. Subscribing to a rigid, absolute, closed belief system

____ 5. Prejudice associated with traditional American moral values and the Protestant Ethic

80

____ 6. A social label or condition that defines a
person as flawed or undesirable

____ 7. A higher-order goal that can be achieved
only if groups cooperate with one another

a. defense mechanisms
b. segregation
c. dogmatism
d. symbolic racism
e. ethnocentrism
f. superordinate goal
g. stigma

MULTIPLE CHOICE QUESTIONS

Circle the one best answer to each question.
Check your responses against the correct answers
at the end of this chapter.

1. Prejudice is
   a. a negative attitude
   b. generally learned
   c. a negative prejudgment of a group
   d. all of the above

2. In the 1954 case <u>Brown v. the Board of
   Education</u>, the U.S. Supreme Court ruled that
   the _____ principle was not legal in the
   public schools.
   a. "separate but equal"
   b. "fairness"
   c. "equity"
   d. "symbolic racism"

3. The _____ was developed as a measure of
   authoritarianism.
   a. F scale
   b. Anti-Semitism scale
   c. Ethnocentrism scale
   d. A scale

4. The _____ theory proposes that people are motivated to evaluate in-groups more positively than out-groups in order to enhance their identity and self-esteem.
   a. intergroup contact
   b. social identity
   c. earned reputation
   d. dogmatism

5. In Sherif's Robber's Cave study, the use of _____ goals helped reduce conflict and prejudice.
   a. in-group
   b. superordinate
   c. competitive
   d. social

6. The intergroup contact hypothesis suggests that contact reduces prejudice if the contact is
   a. socially supported
   b. equal status
   c. in pursuit of common goals
   d. all of the above

7. The _____ component of prejudice is based on the beliefs or stereotypes about groups.
   a. behavioral
   b. affective
   c. cognitive
   d. none of the above

8. Society often treats stigmatized people harshly because
   a. they threaten our accustomed social roles
   b. they make us feel uncomfortable
   c. they remind us of our own frailty and mortality
   d. all of the above

9. Recent summaries of research on school integration have shown _____ results in terms of reducing prejudice and increasing school achievement.
   a. positive
   b. negative
   c. mixed
   d. none of the above

10. Survey research clearly points to _____ as a major cause of residential segregation.
    a. stereotypes
    b. prejudice
    c. authoritarian personality
    d. intergroup cooperation

11. The study by Wilder (1984) suggests that one reason why positive contact with one member of an out-group may not change our attitude toward the group is because
    a. we view the individual as an exception
    b. we view the individual as typical
    c. of the mass media
    d. of our religious beliefs

12. Research suggests that _____ classrooms are effective in increasing positive social interactions between individuals of different groups.
    a. cooperative
    b. competitive
    c. interracial
    d. traditional

ANSWERS TO COMPLETION ITEMS

1. Discrimination (303)
2. sociocultural (305)
3. out; in (310)
4. authoritarian (319-321)
5. just world (324)
6. competition (318-319)
7. contact (331)
8. Stereotypes (307)
9. Minimal (325-326)
10. conservatism (323)

ANSWERS TO MATCHING QUESTIONS

1. b (303)
2. e (310)
3. a (321)
4. c (322)
5. d (323)
6. g (324)
7. f (329)

ANSWERS TO MULTIPLE CHOICE QUESTIONS

1. d (302)
2. a (303)
3. a (319)
4. b (326)
5. b (329)
6. d (331-333)
7. c (302)
8. d (324)
9. c (332)
10. b (337)
11. a (334-336)
12. a (332-333)

CHAPTER 10

GENDER AND SOCIAL BEHAVIOR

CHAPTER OUTLINE

I.   The Changing Roles of Women and Men

II. Psychological Research on Sex and Gender

III. Stereotypes About Women and Men

    A. Personality Stereotypes
    B. Broader Stereotypes About Gender
    C. Gender and the Perception of Ability

IV. Sex Differences

    A. The Study of Sex Differences
       1. The statistical assessment of group
          differences
       2. The evidence for sex differences
    B. The Meaning of Sex Differences

V.   Theories of Gender and Sex-Typing

    A. Biological Theories
    B. Freudian Theory
    C. Social Learning Theories
    D. Cognitive Approaches to Gender
    E. Social Role Theory
    F. Self-Presentation Theory of Gender

VI. Masculinity, Femininity, and Androgyny

    A. Masculinity and Femininity as Separate
       Dimensions
    B. Beyond Masculinity, Femininity, and
       Androgyny

LEARNING OBJECTIVES

After reading and studying Chapter 10, you should be able to answer the following questions.

1. Describe how the roles of women and men have changed in recent years, particularly in the area of work. What roles have not changed? (343-347)

2. What is the difference between the terms sex and gender? How are they defined? (347)

3. What cluster of traits have traditionally been associated with women and men? (347-350)

4. How do gender stereotypes interact with stereotypes of different nationalities? (350-351)

5. What factors or components determine our gender stereotypes? (350-354)

6. When do gender stereotypes affect our evaluation of specific individuals? (353)

7. How do we tend to explain successes differently for men and women? (354-355)

8. Statistically, how do psychologists study and measure sex differences? What is the meaning of the $\underline{d}$ statistic? (357-360)

9. What major sex differences have been supported by meta-analysis? (359-362)

10. List the different theories of gender differences. What kinds of explanations are suggested by the different theories of gender? (363-378)

11. Compare and constrast the biological and Freudian theories of gender. (364-368)

12. What support has been found for the influence of social learning on sex differences and gender-related behavior? (368-370)

13. Describe Kohlberg's cognitive-development theory of gender-related behavior. How does it differ from social learning theory? (370-371)

14. Based on Eagly's social role analysis of gender, how does occupational information affect gender stereotypes? (372-374)

15. What four different components of gender influence our concept of "female" or "male" in everyday life? (376-377)

16. How do traditional masculinity-femininity scales differ from recent scales of masculinity-femininity? (378-381)

17. What is meant by the term androgyny? What are some of the major differences between androgynous people and traditionally masculine or feminine individuals? (380-382)

KEY TERMS TO KNOW

After reading and studying Chapter 10, you should be able to define or understand the following terms.

sex (347)
gender (347)
gender stereotypes (347-353)
sex differences (356-363)
normal distribution (357-359)
mean (357)
standard deviation (358)
d statistic (359-361)
meta-analysis (359-361)
biological theories of gender (364-366)
Freudian theory of gender (366-368)
castration anxiety (367)
Oedipus complex (367)
penis envy (368)
social learning theories of gender (368-370)
cognitive-development theory (370-371)
gender schema theory (371)
social role theory (372-374)
self-presentation theories of gender (375)
gender identity (376-377)
femininity (378-382)
masculinity (378-382)
androgyny (380-382)

COMPLETION ITEMS

Fill in the word(s) to complete each of the following statements. Check your responses against the correct answers at the end of this chapter.

1. Women's work almost always is assigned _____ status than men's work.

2. _____ refers to the biological status of being male or female and _____ refers to social definitions of male or female.

3. Stereotypes of nationality groups resemble the stereotypes of their _____ more than of their _____ .

4. The _____ statistic allows psychologists to systematically study sex differences.

5. According to Bem's gender _____ theory, people learn a complex network of gender-related concepts and symbols from their culture.

6. Sex _____ research attempts to study the ways in which men and women actually are alike and different in their behavior.

7. Most children can correctly identify their gender by age _____ .

8. The percentage of the U.S. work force that is female has steadily _____ over the last century.

9. Research suggests that we tend to attribute men's successes to _____ and women's successes more to luck or _____ .

10. The _____ of a distribution is the arithmetic average of all scores.

11. _____ theories of gender differences focus on heredity and physiology.

MATCHING TERMS AND CONCEPTS

Write the letter of the term or concept from below that best fits the following phrases or sentences. Check your responses against the correct answers at the end of this chapter.

____ 1. An individual's self-definition as male or female

____ 2. Refers to the boy's unconscious feelings of sexual attraction to his mother and his rivalry with his father

____ 3. According to Freud, the prime motivator in women's personalitites

____ 4. Possessing both masculine and feminine traits

____ 5. Argues that gender-related behaviors are a social performance that varies depending on the setting and the social audience

____ 6. An individual's biological status of being male or female

a. Oedipus complex
b. androgyny
c. penis envy
d. self-presentation theory of gender
e. sex
f. gender identity

MULTIPLE CHOICE QUESTIONS

Circle the one best answer to each question. Check your responses against the correct answers at the end of this chapter.

1. Overall in the U.S., the ratio of the median income of working women to that of men is about
   a. 60%   c. 90%
   b. 80%   d. 40%

2. The Eagly and Steggen (1986) study, where subjects were given information about the occupation of a person, suggests that the different _____ for men and women lead to gender stereotypes.
   a. social learning   c. biological genes
   b. social roles   d. gender schemas

3. Judgments of individuals made on the basis of _____ are less influenced by gender stereotypes.
   a. social roles
   b. concrete information
   c. physical characteristics
   d. biological sex

4. Which of the following sex differences have been supported by research?
   a. nonverbal behaviors
   b. physical aggression
   c. group conformity
   d. helping when being watched
   e. all of the above

5. Joe notices that his father likes to shoot real guns and to go hunting. _____ theory would predict that Joe may begin to play with his toy gun and pretend to be hunting.
   a. Sociobiological
   b. Self-presentation
   c. Social learning
   d. all of the above

6. "I am a boy, so I should act like a boy" thinks a five-year-old boy. Which theory best predicts this kind of thought sequence?
   a. cognitive-development theory
   b. social learning theory
   c. Freudian theory
   d. social role theory

7. Research suggests that femininity is positively related to
   a. mental health
   b. performance on mathematics tasks
   c. performance on visual-spatial tasks
   d. success in interpersonal relationships

8. Biological explanations for sex differences are more plausible if sex differences
   a. occur early in development
   b. occur consistently across cultures
   c. occur consistently across species
   d. all of the above

9. _____ are social beliefs about women's and men's personality traits, abilities, social role, physical characteristics, and sexual behavior.
   a. Gender stereotypes
   b. Sex differences
   c. Gender identities
   d. Androgynous feelings

10. In Goldberg's (1968) study where subject rate essays supposedly written by either female or male authors, female subjects rated the essays
    a. attributed to male authors more positively
    b. attributed to female authors more positively
    c. attributed to female authors more positively only on "feminine" topics
    d. none of the above

11. The _____ is a measure of the spread of a distribution.
    a. mean   c. median
    b. <u>d</u> statistic   d. standard deviation

12. Most recent concepts of masculinity-femininity suggest that they are
    a. opposite ends of a single dimension
    b. two independent dimensions
    c. the same thing
    d. based strictly on biological sex

13. A personality trait defined as the degree to which an individual reports possessing instrumental personality traits is
    a. masculinity   c. androgyny
    b. femininity   d. transexuality

14. The cluster of stereotypical traits associated with men are related to _____ traits, while the stereotypical traits associated with women are _____ traits.
    a. instrumental; expressive
    b. expressive; instrumental
    c. instrumental; goal-oriented
    d. nurturing; expressive

ANSWERS TO COMPLETION ITEMS

1. lower   (345)
2. Sex; gender   (347)
3. men; women   (350)
4. <u>d</u>   (359)
5. schema   (371)
6. difference   (347)
7. 2 or 3   (370)
8. increased   (345-347)
9. ability; effort   (354-355)
10. mean   (357)
11. Biological   (364-366)

ANSWERS TO MATCHING QUESTIONS

1. f (376)
2. a (367)
3. c (368)
4. b (380)
5. d (375)

ANSWERS TO MULTIPLE CHOICE QUESTIONS

 1. a (345)
 2. b (372-373)
 3. b (353)
 4. e (361-362)
 5. c (369)
 6. a (371)
 7. d (380)
 8. d (364)
 9. a (348-352)
10. a (354)
11. d (359)
12. b (380-382)
13. a (379-382)
14. a (348-350)

CHAPTER 11

LIKING, LOVING, AND CLOSE RELATIONSHIPS

CHAPTER OUTLINE

I. <u>Trends in the Scientific Study of Attraction</u>

II. <u>The Beginnings of Attraction</u>

    A. Affiliations and Anxiety: The "Dr. Zilstein Experiment"
       1. Reasons for the anxiety-affiliation relationship
    B. From Affiliation to Attraction
       1. Proximity: The architecture of attraction
       2. Mere exposure: I've grown accustomed to your face
       3. Similarity: Birds of a feather
       4. Physical attractiveness

III. <u>Theories of Attraction</u>

    A. Learning Theories
    B. Exchange and Equity Theories
       1. Exchange Theory: The economics of friendship
       2. Equity theory: Investing in love
    C. Cognitive Consistency Theories

IV. <u>Love</u>

    A. The Sociobiological Perspective
       1. The evolutionary origins of love
       2. Are we different from other species?
       3. Sex differences in love and sexuality
    B. The History of Love in Western Culture
    C. The Social Psychology of Love
       1. Three ways of defining love
    D. How Do You Know You're in Love?

V.   The Life Cycle of Close Relationships

    A. Initial Attractions and Beginnings
    B. Building a Relationship
    C. Continuation and Consolidation
        1. Communication in relationships
        2. Communal vs. exchange relationships
        3. External supports
    D. Deterioration and Decline
        1. Alternatives and barriers
        2. Equity and inequity in relationships
        3. Negotiating bad times
    E. Endings

VI. Summary

VII. Glossary

LEARNING OBJECTIVES

After reading and studying Chapter 11, you should be able to answer the following questions.

  1. Describe the trends in the scientific study of attraction. (388-389)

  2. Define affiliation and attraction. Describe Schachter's "Dr. Zilstein Study" of affiliation and anxiety. (389-391)

  3. Explain the relationship between proximity and attraction. How is the mere exposure effect related to the proximity effect? (392-394)

  4. What is the relationship between similarity and attraction? Describe the roommate study by Newcomb (1961). (394-396)

  5. Describe Murstein's three-stage model of attraction. (397)

6. Summarize research dealing with the impact of physical attractiveness on attraction. Does physical attractiveness give any advantages other than popularity? (398-401)

7. Describe how attraction can be understood using learning theories. (401-402)

8. Explain how exchange and equity theories apply to our understanding of attraction. (402-403)

9. How does balance theory explain patterns of likes and dislikes? (404-406)

10. Describe the sociobiological perspective of love. According to this view, what is the major purpose of love? (408-409)

11. Describe some of the historical views of love and sex beginning with the Greeks and Romans. (409-412)

12. How does the sex ratio hypothesis explain the historical variations in attitudes toward love and marriage? (412-413)

13. How do social psychologists empirically measure love? What kinds of attraction are measured by Rubin's scales? (413-417)

14. What are the three main dimensions of love according to Sternberg's model of love? (414-415)

15. What are the six styles of love assessed by Hendrick and Hendrick's love scales? (415-417)

16. According to the two-factor theory of love, how do you know you're in passionate love? (418-421)

17. List and briefly describe Levinger's five stages in the development of close relationships. (421-427)

18. Compare and contrast communal vs. exchange relationships. (424)

19. According to Rusbult and Zembrodt, what are the four common ways of dealing with dissatisfaction in relationships? (426)

KEY TERMS TO KNOW

After reading and studying Chapter 11, you should be able to define or understand the following terms.

affiliation (389)
attraction (389)
social comparison theory (390)
proximity (392)
mere exposure effect (393)
similarity principle (394)
assortative mating (394)
stimulus-value-role model (397)
learning theories of love (401-402)
exchange theory (402)
comparison level (402)
comparison level for alternatives (403)
equity theory (403)
balance theory (404)
sociobiological theory of love (408-409)
pair-bonding (408)
sex ratio hypothesis (412-413)
social penetration theory (421)
self-disclosure (422)
communal vs. exchange relationships (424)

COMPLETION ITEMS

Fill in the word(s) to complete each of the following statements. Check your responses against the correct answers at the end of this chapter.

1. Research indicates that _____ seem to suffer more disruption from breakups than do _____ .

2. Social psychology has focused more on the _____ stages of friendships and romantic attractions.

3. Murstein's stage model of attraction begins with the _____ stage, moves to the _____ stage, and finally ends with the _____ stage.

4. According Byrne (1971), the more attitudinal similarity, the _____ the attraction.

5. Attractive people are _____ likely to get caught and reported as criminals than are unattractive people.

6. _____ theory suggests that we tend to choose those relationships that are most profitable.

7. According to social penetration theory, the inital stages of close relationships are characterized by self-_____ and social _____ .

8. _____ relationships are characterized by a careful tally of costs and rewards and an expectation of exact reciprocity, while _____ relationships are more concerned with the partner's well-being and needs.

9. According to Berscheid and Walster, to experience passionate love, you must experience physiological _____, and you must _____ it as being due to love.

MATCHING TERMS AND CONCEPTS

Write the letter of the term or concept from below that best fits the following phrases or sentences. Check your responses against the correct answers at the end of this chapter.

____ 1. Misery loves miserable company.

____ 2. Refers to a positive attitude or emotion we feel toward another person

____ 3. Relationships characterized by concern with the partner's well-being

____ 4. I've grown accustomed to your face.

____ 5. People mate in nonrandom ways usually based on similarity.

____ 6. Focuses on the consistency of our likes and dislikes

____ 7. Intense emotional attachments with others

____ 8. Adrenaline makes the heart grow fonder.

a. two-component theory of emotion
b. mere exposure effect
c. affiliation-anxiety relationship
d. assortative mating
e. balance theory
f. communal relationships
g. pair-bonding
h. attraction

MULTIPLE CHOICE QUESTIONS

Circle the one best answer to each question.
Check your responses against the correct answers
at the end of this chapter.

1. According to the "Dr. Zilstein study," we are
   more likely to affiliate when we are
   a. socially embarrassed
   b. exposed to a repeated stimulus
   c. anxious or fearful
   d. all of the above

2. Which of the following is <u>not</u> one of the
   major stages in Murstein's model of
   attraction?
   a. stimulus   c. role
   b. value   d. deterioration

3. The tendency for people who live or work near
   each other to develop an attraction to each
   other is consistent with the _____ effect.
   a. proximity   c. similarity
   b. balance   d. exchange

4. In the computer dating study by Walster and
   associates (1966), the only strong factor
   that influenced attraction was
   a. similarity
   b. physical attractiveness
   c. proximity
   d. mere exposure

5. We tend to like people more when they are
   associated with pleasure, and less when they
   are associated with pain or costs. This
   statement is best explained by _____
   theory.
   a. social penetration
   b. equity
   c. learning
   d. balance

6. According to exchange theory, we compare the costs and rewards of a relationship to a(n)
   a. comparison level
   b. comparison level for alternatives
   c. ideal standard
   d. both a and b

7. _____ argue(s) that romantic love and pair-bonding serve the purpose of binding together family units to nurture helpless infants.
   a. Learning theories
   b. Sociobiological theory
   c. Balance theory
   d. Exchange theory

8. The principle of _____ suggests that each partner should receive profits from a relationship in proportion to their investment.
   a. similarity   c. proximity
   b. pair-bonding   d. equity

9. Which of the following is not one of Sternberg's main dimensions of love?
   a. liking   c. intimacy
   b. passion   d. commitment

10. _____ refers to the desire or motivation to be with others, regardless of liking.
    a. Attraction   c. Pair-bonding
    b. Affiliation   d. Love

11. In comparison to less physically attractive people, physically attractive people are
    a. less popular
    b. rated better on written work
    c. treated less leniently in the courtroom
    d. rated by teachers as less intelligent

12. Two constructive ways of dealing with
    dissatisfaction in relationships are
    a. voice and loyalty   c. exit and neglect
    b. neglect and loyalty d. exit and voice

ANSWERS TO COMPLETION ITEMS

1. men; women (427)
2. early or initial (388)
3. stimulus; value; role (397)
4. greater (396)
5. less (400)
6. Exchange (402)
7. disclosure; exchange (421-422)
8. Exchange; communal (424)
9. arousal; label (418-419)

ANSWERS TO MATCHING QUESTIONS

1. c (389-391)
2. h (389)
3. f (424)
4. b (393-394)
5. d (394)
6. e (404-405)
7. g (408)
8. a (418-419)

ANSWERS TO MULTIPLE CHOICE QUESTIONS

1. c (390-391)   7. b (408)
2. d (397)   8. d (403)
3. a (392)   9. a (414-415)
4. b (398)   10. b (389)
5. c (401)   11. b (400)
6. d (402-403)   12. a (426)

CHAPTER 12

AGGRESSION

CHAPTER OUTLINE

I. <u>Aggression</u>

    A. Defining Aggression
    B. Measuring Aggression

II. <u>Factors That Influence Human Aggression</u>

    A. Biological Groups, Instincts, and Aggression
    B. Cultural Influences on Aggression
    C. Individual Differences in Aggression
       1. Aggressiveness as a trait
       2. Physiology and aggression
    D. The Environment, Internal Psychological Processes, and Aggression
       1. Aggression as a response to aggression
       2. Physical pain and aggression
       3. Heat and aggression
       4. Frustration and aggression
       5. Arousal and aggression
    E. Social Learning and Aggression
       1. The mass media and aggression
       2. The effects of TV violence on children
       3. Media sex and aggression
       4. Sexual violence

III. <u>Reducing Aggression</u>

    A. Catharsis
    B. Punishing Aggression
    C. Creating Responses Incompatible with Aggression
    D. Providing Social Restraints
    E. Cognitive Strategies for Controlling Aggression

F. A Concluding Word on Controlling
   Aggression

IV. Summary

V. Glossary

LEARNING OBJECTIVES

After reading and studying Chapter 12, you should
be able to answer the following questions.

1. How do social psychologists define
   aggression? Compare and contrast hostile and
   instrumental aggression. (435-436)

2. Describe how psychologists measure
   aggression. How valid are the experimental
   measures of aggression compared to aggression
   in everyday life? (436)

3. List some of the major factors that influence
   human aggression. (437-463)

4. Describe the instinct theories of aggression
   proposed by Freud and Lorenz. Why are these
   theories scientifically rejected by social
   psychologists? (437-439)

5. Summarize some of the individual differences
   in aggression. Is the trait of
   aggressiveness stable over time? (440-442)

6. What is the relationship between physical
   pain and aggression? (442-444)

7. Describe the original frustration-aggression
   hypothesis. What does current research
   suggest about the relationship between
   frustration and aggression? (444-448)

8. What does Davies's "J-curve" theory of social revolution suggest about frustration and societal aggression? (446-447)

9. What factors may account for the relationship between arousal and aggression? (449)

10. Describe the social learning perspective of aggression. What learning principles seem to apply to understanding aggression? (449-463)

11. What is the weapons effect? What factors seem to account for its influence? (452)

12. Summarize the findings on the impact of TV violence on aggression. How violent is TV programming in the U.S.? (451-456)

13. What are some of the effects of media sex on attitudes and aggression? Is the availability of pornography associated with sexual violence? (456-463)

14. What are some of the major strategies that have been suggested or studied for reducing aggressive behavior? (464-473)

15. What is meant by the concept of catharsis? What does research show about the effectiveness of catharsis as a strategy for reducing aggression? (464-466)

16. Under what conditions is punishment or the threat of punishment more likely to be effective in reducing violence? (466-467)

17. What do psychologists mean by an incompatible response? What are some examples of incompatible responses to aggression? (467)

18. What can be done to prevent family violence? Briefly describe three levels of prevention programs that can help in reducing such violence. (468-471)

19. Briefly describe some of the cognitive strategies being used to reduce the impact of violent TV programming. (472-473)

KEY TERMS TO KNOW

After reading and studying Chapter 12, you should be able to define or understand the following terms.

war (434)
aggression (435)
hostile aggression (435)
instrumental aggression (436)
"aggression machine" (436)
instinct theory of aggression (437-439)
catharsis hypothesis (438)
testosterone (442)
frustration-aggression hypothesis (444-448)
J-curve theory of social revolutions (446-447)
relative deprivation (446-447)
social learning theory (449-451)
instrumental conditioning (450-451)
weapons effect (452)
rape myths (461)
punishment (466-467)
incompatible responses (467)
primary, secondary, and tertiary prevention (468)

COMPLETION ITEMS

Fill in the word(s) to complete each of the following statements. Check your responses against the correct answers at the end of this chapter.

1. _____ is behavior directed against another living being that is _____ to harm or injure.

2. _____ theories often propose universal aggressive impulses for all people.

3. Research indicates that an individual's general level of aggression is relatively _____ and _____ over time.

4. Some studies suggest a relationship between the sex hormone _____ and aggression.

5. Frustration may influence aggression simply because it leads to general _____, which energizes aggressive behavior.

6. The principle of _____ conditioning suggests that aggression is learned through positive and negative reinforcement.

7. Punishment works best to control _____ aggression rather than _____ aggression.

8. _____ prevention techniques are designed to prevent family violence before it starts.

9. Studies show that _____ pornography can increase aggression, particularly by _____ against _____.

10. Humor, empathy, or mild sexual arousal may reduce aggression because they create _____ responses with aggression.

MATCHING TERMS AND CONCEPTS

Write the letter of the term or concept from below that best fits the following phrases or sentences. Check your responses against the correct answers at the end of this chapter.

___ 1. Institutionalized aggression conducted by groups, usually nation-states

___ 2. Aggression that is generally provoked by pain, upset, or frustration

___ 3. Nonemotional aggression performed to gain a desired reward

___ 4. Interference with the occurrence of a goal-response

___ 5. The gap between reality and expectations of social standards

___ 6. The venting of aggressive impulses through fantasy, exercise, and verbal aggression

___ 7. Delivering an aversive stimulus after an undesired behavior

a. instrumental aggression
b. relative deprivation
c. hostile aggression
d. war
e. catharsis
f. frustration
g. punishment

MULTIPLE CHOICE QUESTIONS

Circle the one best answer to each question.
Check your responses against the correct answers
at the end of this chapter.

1. One of major problems with the instinct
   theory of aggression is that the explanation
   is
   a. based on rewards and punishments
   b. circular
   c. based on learned behaviors
   d. based on personality influences

2. The _____ hypothesis suggests that by
   venting their aggression through fantasy,
   exercise, etc., people display less
   aggression later on.
   a. frustration-aggression
   b. instinct-aggression
   c. catharsis
   d. arousal-aggression

3. Research consistently shows that people
   respond to attacks with
   a. reciprocity or counterattacks
   b. frustration
   c. catharsis
   d. a decrease in arousal

4. The _____ theory suggests that social
   revolutions are most likely to occur when a
   period of economic development is followed by
   a short period of sharp reversal.
   a. frustration-aggression
   b. J-curve
   c. social learning
   d. arousal-aggression

5. Studies by Donnerstein and others confirm
that sexual _____ can contribute to
aggression.
   a. inhibition   c. catharsis
   b. arousal   d. all of the above

6. To be effective in reducing aggressive
behavior, punishment should be
   a. relatively strong
   b. applied quickly and consistently
   c. contingent upon bad aggressive behavior
   d. all of the above

7. _____ prevention is designed to treat
recurring and ongoing family violence
   a. Primary   c. Tertiary
   b. Secondary   d. none of the above

8. The level of violence in TV programs in the
U.S.
   a. is very high
   b. has remained relatively constant over the
      past 20 yerars
   c. is particularly high in cartoons
   d. all of the above

9. Violent pornography
   a. may reduce aggressive behavior through
      "catharsis"
   b. is not associated with male violence
   c. can lead men to endorse "rape myths"
   d. all of the above

10. In a longitudinal study on the effects of TV
viewing, Huesmann (1986) found that viewing
violent TV at age 8
   a. was not related to aggressive behavior in
      adulthood
   b. was related to criminal behavior at age 30
   c. later decreased adult aggressive behavior
   d. increased aggressive behavior in girls but
      not boys

11. Which of the following factors seems to increase the level of aggression and violence?
    a. pain
    b. marijuana
    c. empathy
    d. all of the above

12. The _____ effect occurs because certain stimuli frequently associated with aggression may become learned aggressive cues.
    a. frustration
    b. weapons
    c. catharsis
    d. instrumental

13. The _____ hypothesis suggests that interfering with a goal-response always leads to aggression.
    a. frustration-aggression
    b. arousal-aggression
    c. catharsis
    d. weapons

ANSWERS TO COMPLETION ITEMS

1. Aggression; intended (435)
2. Instinct (437-439)
3. consistent; stable (440)
4. testosterone (442)
5. arousal (449)
6. instrumental or operant (450-451)
7. instrumental; hostile (466)
8. Primary (468-470)
9. violent; males; females (459-463)
10. incompatible (467)

ANSWERS TO MATCHING QUESTIONS

1. d (434)
2. c (435)
3. a (436)
4. f (444)
5. b (446-447)
6. e (438)
7. g (466)

ANSWERS TO MULTIPLE CHOICE QUESTIONS

```
 1.  b   (437)
 2.  c   (438)
 3.  a   (442)
 4.  b   (446-447)
 5.  b   (449)
 6.  d   (466-467)
 7.  c   (468-470)
 8.  d   (453)
 9.  c   (456-463)
10.  b   (456-457)
11.  a   (442-443)
12.  b   (452-453)
13.  a   (445)
```

CHAPTER 13

ALTRUISM AND PROSOCIAL BEHAVIOR

CHAPTER OUTLINE

I. Defining and Measuring Prosocial Behavior

II. Major Approaches to the Study of Prosocial
    Behavior

    A. Sociobiological Theory and Prosocial
    Behavior
       1. Kin selection
       2. Reciprocal altruism
    B. Cultural Norms of Prosocial Behavior
       1. Social norms
       2. The limitations of normative approaches

III. The Psychology of Prosocial Behavior

    A. Is There a Prosocial Personality?
       1. The development of prosocial behavior
    B. The Psychology of Emergency Intervention
       1. Latané and Darley's cognitive model
       2. The bystander effect
       3. Emotional arousal and perceived cost as
          factors
       4. Misattribution of arousal
       5. Pure altruism: Fact or fantasy?
    C. Guilt, Moods, and Helping
       1. Guilt
       2. Bad moods and helping
       3. Good moods and helping

IV. Helping People to Help

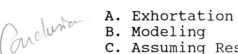

    A. Exhortation
    B. Modeling
    C. Assuming Responsibility
    D. Humanizing the Victim Who Needs Help

E. Education About Helping

V. Summary

VI. Glossary

LEARNING OBJECTIVES

After reading and studying Chapter 13, you should be able to answer the following questions.

1. Define prosocial and altruistic behavior. Compare and constrast these two terms. (478-480)

2. What are some ways to measure prosocial behavior? (480)

3. List and briefly discuss the major approaches to the study of prosocial behavior. (480-487)

4. Summarize the sociobiological theory of prosocial behavior. Why is prosocial behavior considered to be adaptive? (482-485)

5. List and briefly describe the three most prominent norms governing prosocial behavior? (485-487)

6. What are some of the factors that lead to the development of prosocial behaviors in children? (489-491)

7. What are the five cognitive steps in Latané and Darley's decision model of emergency intervention? (492-493)

8. What is the bystander effect? What are some of the situational factors that affect emergency intervention? (492-497)

9. According Piliavin, Dovidio, Gaertner, and Clark (1981), what factors lead individuals to intervene in emergencies and what are the causal links among factors? (497-498)

10. How does the perceived cost for helping and not helping affect our willingness to intervene in an emergency? (499-502)

11. How do attributions of arousal affect our behavior in ambiguous and unambiguous emergency situations? (503-504)

12. According to Batson and his colleagues, do people ever show pure altruism? What is the relationship between empathy and altruism? (503-505)

13. When and why does guilt motivate prosocial behavior? (507-508)

14. What is the effect of good and bad moods on prosocial behavior? How long does the effect last? (508-511)

15. Why are some people uncomfortable about receiving help? (512)

16. Describe several common techniques to increase helping behavior. (513-517)

KEY TERMS TO KNOW

After reading and studying Chapter 13, you should be able to define or understand the following terms.

prosocial behavior (478)
emergency intervention (478)
altruism (480)
pure and pseudo altruism (480)
kin selection (482)
reciprocal altruism (483)
tit for tat (483)
social norms (485)
norm of reciprocity (485)
norm of equity (486)
norm of social responsibility (486)
bystander effect (492)
diffusion of responsibility (497)
guilt (507)
moral exhortation (513)

COMPLETION ITEMS

Fill in the word(s) to complete each of the
following statements. Check your responses
against the correct answers at the end of this
chapter.

1. _____ _____ is behavior that
   intentionally helps or benefits another
   person.

2. The norm of _____ prescribes that
   people should help and not hurt those who
   have helped them

3. According to Daniel Batson, pure altruism may
   have its basis in our feelings of _____.

4. _____ of responsibility is one
   explanation for the bystander effect.

5. _____ selection is the process by which
   natural selection favors animals that promote
   the survivial of genetically related
   individuals.

6. _____ moods consistently lead to more helping and prosocial behavior.

7. Evolutionary theories do not predict _____ altruism.

8. Research shows that prosocial behavior can be encouraged by _____ models.

9. Research suggests that _____ television may have a greater impact than _____ television on children.

10. Equity, reciprocity, and social responsibility are all examples of _____.

MATCHING TERMS AND CONCEPTS

Write the letter of the term or concept from below that best fits the following phrases or sentences. Check your responses against the correct answers at the end of this chapter.

____ 1. Quick helping in response to sudden events that endanger another person

____ 2. Helping another person for no reward and even at some cost to oneself

____ 3. Behavior that benefits another with the proviso that the other is expected to return the favor

____ 4. People should give aid to a dependent person in proportion to his or her need.

____ 5. The tendency to feel less personal responsibility for helping when in the presence of others

____ 6. A negative emotion that occurs when individuals believe they have committed a moral transgression

____ 7. Verbally urging others to help and to live according to moral principles

a. altruism
b. reciprocal altruism
c. norm of social responsibility
d. diffusion of responsibility
e. guilt
f. emergency intervention
g. moral exhortation

MULTIPLE CHOICE QUESTIONS

Circle the one best answer to each question. Check your responses against the correct answers at the end of this chapter.

1. Research indicates that impulsive helping is most likely to occur when the
   a. emergency is quite clear
   b. emergency occurs in a real-life setting
   c. helper has some prior relationship with the victim
   d. all of the above

2. The "tit-for-tat" strategy in prosocial behavior is a good illustration of _____.
   a. the norm of social responsibility
   b. reciprocal altruism
   c. the norm of equity
   d. moral exhortation

3. Which of the following helping behaviors has been observed in whales and dolphins?
   a. standing by
   b. assistance
   c. support
   d. all of the above

4. According to Latané and Darley's decision model of emergency intervention, the first step is to
   a. take responsibility
   b. define the situation as an emergency
   c. notice that something is wrong
   d. decide how to help

5. People in bad moods help more if
   a. they are not observed by other people
   b. they think that helping will improve their own mood
   c. they are in a competitive situation
   d. all of the above

6. The presence of other bystanders often inhibits people from helping in emergencies. This is called the
   a. norm of irresponsibility
   b. tit-for-tat strategy
   c. bystander effect
   d. pseudoaltruism effect

7. Research by Batson and his colleagues suggests that people _____ are more likely to help even if they can escape the situation.
   a. high on diffusion of responsibility
   b. high in empathy
   c. low on guilt
   d. low on masculinity

8. In the "subway" study by Piliavin and
   Piliavin (1972), people were less likely to
   help a stranger who collapsed when
   a. blood came from the man's mouth
   b. when the stranger was a female
   c. the costs for helping were low
   d. few people were present

9. Research indicates that females are _____
   likely than (as) males to help when the
   victim is a woman.
   a. much more
   b. as
   c. less
   d. slightly more

10. Latané and Darley's "smoke-filled room"
    experiment found that people reported the
    smoke more quickly when
    a. alone
    b. with two passive confederates
    c. with two other naive subjects
    d. none of the above

11. People who misattribute their arousal during
    an ambiguous emergency are _____ likely to
    help.
    a. less
    b. as
    c. slightly more
    d. more

12. Which of the following techniques have been
    used to increase helping behavior?
    a. moral exhortation
    b. prosocial models
    c. assigning responsibility
    d. all of the above

ANSWERS TO COMPLETION ITEMS

1. Prosocial behavior (478)
2. reciprocity (485)
3. empathy (503-506)
4. Diffusion (497)
5. Kin (482)
6. Good (509)
7. pure (485)
8. prosocial (515)
9. prosocial; antisocial (490-491)
10. social or cultural norms (485-487)

ANSWERS TO MATCHING QUESTIONS

1. f (478)
2. a (480)
3. b (483)
4. c (486)
5. d (497)
6. e (507)
7. g (513)

ANSWERS TO MULTIPLE CHOICE QUESTIONS

1. d (479)
2. b (483)
3. d (484)
4. c (492-493)
5. b (509)
6. c (492)
7. b (503-506)
8. a (500)
9. c (489)
10. a (492-495)
11. a (503-504)
12. d (513)

CHAPTER 14

CONFORMITY, COMPLIANCE, AND OBEDIENCE

CHAPTER OUTLINE

I. Social Influence

   A. Kinds of Social Influence
   B. Levels of Social Influence

II. Conformity

   A. Research on Conformity
      1. Sherif and the autokinetic effect
      2. Asch's minority of one against a
         unanimous majority
   B. Factors That Influence Conformity
      1. Personality
      2. Gender
      3. Group size
      4. Group attractiveness and cohesiveness
      5. Status in the group
      6. Social support: The presence of other
         nonconformists
      7. Commitment and conformity
      8. Minority influence

III. Compliance

   A. Positive Moods and Compliance
   B. Reciprocity and Compliance
   C. Commitment and Compliance
   D. Psychological Reactance and Compliance

IV. Obedience

   A. The Nature of Obedience
      1. Institutional setting and obedience
      2. Social pressures and obedience

3. The role of the person giving and
     receiving commands
   B. The Milgram Studies in Perspective
   C. Obedience Studies Since Milgram's

V.   Resisting Social Influence

VI. Summary

VII. Glossary

LEARNING OBJECTIVES

After reading and studying Chapter 14, you should
be able to answer the following questions.

1. What are the major kinds of social influence?
   Give an example of each. (522)

2. Describe the three different levels of social
   influence identified by Kelman (1958). (523)

3. Define conformity. Describe Sherif's
   autokinetic method of measuring conformity.
   What were the results of his studies on the
   persistence of norms? (524-526)

4. How did Solomon Asch measure conformity and
   what were the major results of his studies?
   (526-529)

5. What are some of the major factors that
   influence conformity? (529-545)

6. What is the effect of personality on
   conformity? (530)

7. Summarize the studies on gender differences
   in conformity. How does Eagly's social-role
   theory explain these differences? (530-531)

8. How are the size of influencing groups and the size of the target groups related to conformity and social influence? (531-533)

9. Describe the Bennington College study by Newcomb (1943). What was the effect of reference groups on attitude change? (534-535)

10. How does status within a group affect our tendency to conform? (534-537)

11. How does social support and commitment to a nonconforming response affect conformity? (537-539)

12. Describe the diamond model of social influence. (540-541)

13. When is a minority most likely to influence a majority? (542-545)

14. Define and give several examples of compliance. What strategies make us more likely to comply with others' requests? (545-551)

15. Briefly describe and give an example of the following compliance strategies: positive moods, ingratiation, and doing favors. (546)

16. Compare and contrast the door-in-the face and the that's-not-all techniques. (548)

17. Describe some of the brainwashing techniques used by the Chinese during the Korean War on American prisoners of war. How successful was the brainwashing? (552-553)

18. How does obedience differ from conformity and compliance? (554)

19. Describe the method used by Milgram to study obedience. What factors make us more or less likely to engage in destructive obedience? (554-560)

20. How can people resist social influence? (560-562)

KEY TERMS TO KNOW

After reading and studying Chapter 14, you should be able to define or understand the following terms.

doublethink (521)
social influence (522)
conformity (522)
compliance (522)
obedience (522)
autokinetic effect (524)
normative social influence (528)
informational social influence (528)
deviate, slider, mode (529)
social influence model (531)
group cohesiveness (532-534)
reference group (534-535)
nonconformists (537)
diamond model (540-541)
congruence (540-541)
anticonformity (540)
self-anticonformity (540-541)
minority influence (542-545)
double minority (542)
private acceptance vs. public compliance (543)
ingratiation (546)
norm of reciprocity (546-548)
door-in-the face technique (548)
that's-not-all technique (548)
foot-in-the-door technique (549)
low-ball technique (549-550)
reactance (550)

brainwashing (552-553)
luncheon technique (561)

COMPLETION ITEMS

Fill in the word(s) to complete each of the
following statements. Check your responses
against the correct answers at the end of this
chapter.

1. People _____ when they maintain or
   change their behavior to be consistent with
   group standards; they _____ when they
   accede to a request made by another; and they
   _____ when they follow a direct command
   from a legitimate authority.

2. Sherif's research showed that when asked to
   make ambiguous perceptual judgments, people
   _____ to emerging social _____
   or standards.

3. People conform to be liked (_____
   social influence), and to be correct
   (_____ social influence).

4. The Bennington College study by Newcomb
   (1943) showed that we conform more to groups
   we are _____ to.

5. The more that people commit themselves to a
   nonconforming response, the _____ they will
   stick to it in the face of group _____.

6. Minorities are more likely to influence
   _____ attitudes, whereas majorities
   are more likely to influence _____
   attitudes.

7. Research supports the idea that _____ moods aid us in gaining compliance from others.

MATCHING TERMS AND CONCEPTS

Write the letter of the term or concept from below that best fits the following phrases or sentences. Check your responses against the correct answers at the end of this chapter.

_____ 1. Acceding to a request made by another person

_____ 2. The strategy of saying pleasant things to another in order to gain compliance

_____ 3. The strategy of offering a product at a high price and then improving the deal before the target has a chance to refuse

_____ 4. Following a direct commmand, typically from someone perceived to be a legitimate authority

_____ 5. The strategy of following a small initial request with a much larger second request

_____ 6. Maintaining or changing behavior to be consistent with group standards

_____ 7. Getting a target to comply by threatening his or her freedom of choice, sometimes by creating an illusion of scarcity

a. that's-not-all technique
b. compliance
c. foot-in-the-door technique
d. conformity
e. ingratiation
f. reactance
g. obedience

MULTIPLE CHOICE QUESTIONS

Circle the one best answer to each question.
Check your responses against the correct answers
at the end of this chapter.

1. In Asch's original conformity experiments,
   _____ of the subjects conformed at least
   once.
   a. 10%   c. 50%
   b. 25%   d. 75%

2. Groups are termed _____ when all members
   on average are attracted to the group.
   a. cohesive   c. public
   b. high status   d. obedient

3. A car salesperson who gets a customer to
   agree to buy a car with many free options
   "thrown in," and then later informs the
   customer that not all of the options are
   included, is using the _____technique.
   a. foot-in-the-door
   b. door-in-the-face
   c. low-ball
   d. that's-not-all

4. Which of the following is not one of the
   basic kinds of social influence?
   a. conformity
   b. compliance
   c. obedience
   d. none of the above

5. Asch found that if subjects could write their judgments rather than publicly announce them, then
   a. conformity increased
   b. conformity decreased
   c. conformity remained the same
   d. none of the above

6. Which of the following factors increases the likelihood that a minority will influence a majority?
   a. The minority consistently argues their position.
   b. The minority is seen as rigid.
   c. The minority position goes against prevailing cultural norms and trends.
   d. The minority is a double minority.

7. Milgram's research indicates that obedience to an authority increases when
   a. the victim is closer to the subject
   b. the experimenter or authority is farther away
   c. when other members of group have obeyed
   d. all of the above

8. In the diamond model of social influence, _____ refers to agreement between the subject and the group after social influence.
   a. anti-conformity
   b. self-conformity
   c. congruence
   d. independence

9. Research by Asch and others indicates that as group size increases, the percentage of subjects that conforms
   a. increases and then levels off
   b. continues to increase until conformity reaches 100%
   c. increases and then decreases significantly
   d. decreases steadily

10. In Schachter's (1951) "Johnny Rocco" study, the discussion group disliked the _____ group member the most.
    a. mode
    b. slider
    c. deviate
    d. none of the above

11. Conformity in Sherif's autokinetic studies was mainly due to _____ social influence while conformity in Asch's experiments was due more to _____ social influence.
    a. normative; informational
    b. conformity; compliance
    c. informational; normative
    d. public; private

12. The basic finding of Milgram's original obedience study was that _____ of the subjects obeyed and delivered the maximum shock level.
    a. 1%
    b. 25%
    c. 65%
    d. 95%

13. The key in doing small favors (e.g., free samples) to get people to comply with a later request is the norm of
    a. social influence
    b. reciprocity
    c. obedience
    d. conformity

14. The study by Dittes and Kelley (1956) found that _____ status group members are most likely to conform.
    a. high
    b. low
    c. average or marginal
    d. none of the above; status made no difference

ANSWERS TO COMPLETION ITEMS

1. conform; comply; obey (522)
2. conform; norms (524-526)
3. normative; informational (528)
4. attracted (534-535)
5. more; pressure (538-539)
6. private; public (543-545)
7. positive (546)

ANSWERS TO MATCHING QUESTIONS

1. b (522)
2. e (546)
3. a (548)
4. g (522)
5. c (549)
6. d (522)
7. f (550)

ANSWERS TO MULTIPLE CHOICE QUESTIONS

 1. d (527)
 2. a (532-534)
 3. c (549)
 4. d (522)
 5. b (528)
 6. a (542)
 7. c (554-559)
 8. c (540-541)
 9. a (531-533)
10. c (529)
11. c (528)
12. c (554)
13. b (546)
14. c (534-536)

CHAPTER 15

GROUPS

CHAPTER OUTLINE

I. <u>What Is a Group?</u>

II. <u>Studying Group Behavior</u>

    A. Dimensions of Group Behavior

III. <u>Groups at Work</u>

    A. Social Facilitation
    B. Individual Versus Group Performance
       1. Steiner's analysis of group tasks
       2. Social loafing
    C. Decision Making in Groups
       1. Group polarization
    D. Groupthink

IV. <u>Leadership in Groups</u>

    A. What Is Leadership?
    B. Theories of Leadership
       1. The trait approach to leadership
       2. The situational approach to leadership
       3. Fiedler's contingency approach to
          leadership

V. <u>The Good and Bad of Groups</u>

    A. Deindividuation
       1. Deindividuation and self-awareness

VI. <u>Competition and Cooperation in Groups</u>

    A. Cooperation and Competition in
       Experimental Games
       1. The Prisoner's Dilemma

2. The Commons Dilemma

VII. Groups: A Final Word

VIII. Summary

IX. Glossary

LEARNING OBJECTIVES

After reading and studying Chapter 15, you should be able to answer the following questions.

1. How do psychologists define a group? What are some of the important characteristics of people in groups? (568)

2. What are the three main dimensions of group behavior? What are the two fundamental functions of groups and group behavior? (570-571)

3. How does the presence of others affect our performance on tasks? Why is the mere presence of others arousing? (571-575)

4. Accord to Steiner, what are four common kinds of group tasks, and how do they differ from one another? (577-579)

5. Summarize the research findings on social loafing. Why does it occur, and how can it be reduced? (579-583)

6. Describe the group brainstorming method designed by Osborn (1957). How effective is brainstorming? (582)

7. Describe what is meant by group polarization in group decision making. Why does it occur? (583-585)

8. According to Janis's model, what are the causes and consequences of groupthink? How can groups guard against groupthink? (585-588)

9. What is leadership? What are the two main kinds of behavior that leaders engage in? (588-589)

10. Compare and contrast the trait, situational, and contingency approaches to leadership. (589-593)

11. According to French and Raven (1959), what are the five different kinds of power used by leaders? Give an example of each kind of power. (590)

12. According to research by Fiedler, when are task-oriented or socioemotional leaders most effective? (592-594)

13. Define the concept of deindividuation. What factors are more likely to foster deindividuation in groups? (595-601)

14. What two main dimensions distinguish deindividuated people from individuated people? (599-601)

15. What is a mass psychogenic illness? When is it most likely to occur in the workplace? (598-599)

16. Describe the original Prisoner's Dilemma scenario. What factors are likely to lead to cooperative and competitive behavior in the Prisoner's Dilemma game? (602-605)

17. Describe the "tragedy of the commons" dilemma. How can we avoid or prevent such commons dilemmas? (605-607)

KEY TERMS TO KNOW

After reading and studying Chapter 15, you should be able to define or understand the following terms.

group (568)
group outcomes (569)
group processes (569)
Interaction Process Analysis (570)
activity, likability, and task ability (570-571)
social facilitation effect (572-575)
mere presence of others (574)
additive tasks (577-578)
conjunctive tasks (577-578)
disjunctive tasks (577-578)
divisible tasks (577-579)
social loafing (579-581)
pseudogroups (579)
Ringelmann effect (579-580)
brainstorming (582)
nominal group technique (582)
group polarization (583-585)
informational influence (584)
social comparison processes (584)
groupthink (585-588)
mindguards (587)
leadership (588-593)
task specialists (589)
socioemotional leaders (589)
trait approach to leadership (589)
reward power (590)
coercive power (590)
legitimate power (590)
referent power (590)
expert power (590)
situational approach to leadership (591)
contingency model of leadership (592)
Least Preferred Coworker Scale (592)
deindividuation (596-601)
mass psychogenic illness (598-599)
self-awareness (599-601)

COMPLETION ITEMS

Fill in the word(s) to complete each of the
following statements. Check your responses
against the correct answers at the end of this
chapter.

1. A(n) _____ is a collection of
   individuals who interact and communicate with
   one another over a period of time.

2. The three main dimensions of group behavior
   are general _____, _____,
   and _____ ability.

3. The mere _____ of others is arousing,
   and this arousal facilitates _____,
   well-learned responses.

4. _____ is a technique to foster
   creativity in groups.

5. The contingency model proposes that
   _____-oriented leaders are most
   effective in very favorable or very
   unfavorable conditions, whereas the
   _____ leaders are more
   effective in moderately favorable conditions.

6. Group _____ refer to the ongoing
   communications and interactions among group
   members that lead to group outcomes.

7. A social _____ is a situation in which seemingly rational behavior leading to short-term gains for individuals results ultimately in collective ruin.

8. _____ are leaders who excels at task-oriented but not socioemotional skills.

9. Group _____ occurs when group discussion leads group members to more extreme decisions.

10. Groups sometimes develop _____guards whose job is to protect the group from unwelcomed information.

MATCHING TERMS AND CONCEPTS

Write the letter of the term or concept from below that best fits the following phrases or sentences. Check your responses against the correct answers at the end of this chapter.

____ 1. A task (tug-of-war) in which individuals pool or add their efforts

____ 2. A task (relay race) in which individual group members all perform the same subtask(s)

____ 3. A task (jury) in which the group members collaborate to arrive at an "either/or" or "yes/no" decision

____ 4. A task (football team) in which different group members perform different subtasks

____ 5. A disinhibited state that occurs when people lose their individual identities in group settings

_____ 6. An illness of psychological origin that occurs in group settings due to hysterical contagion

_____ 7. A syndrome of bad decison making in cohesive groups

a. divisible
b. additive task
c. disjunctive
d. mass psychogenic illness
e. conjunctive task
f. groupthink
g. deindividuation

MULTIPLE CHOICE QUESTIONS

Circle the one best answer to each question. Check your responses against the correct answers at the end of this chapter.

1. Which of the following is characteristic of people in groups?
   a. they frequently interact
   b. they typically share norms
   c. they perceive themselves part of the group with the same goals
   d. all of the above

2. Zajonc (1965) believes that the mere presence of others produces _____, which leads to social facilitation if the response is well learned.
   a. arousal
   b. fear
   c. activity
   d. a group response

3. _____ are people who strive to maximize the joint profits for themselves and their partner in games such as the Prisoner's Dilemma.
   a. Competitors
   b. Cooperators
   c. Individualists
   d. Mindguards

4. Which of the following is <u>not</u> one of the major dimensions of group behavior?
   a. general activity
   b. brainstorming
   c. likability
   d. task ability

5. _____ occurs when people exert less individual effort when in groups than when alone.
   a. Groupthink
   b. Group polarization
   c. Social loafing
   d. A social trap

6. Which of the following is one of French and Raven's (1959) different kinds of power(s)?
   a. reward and coercive power
   b. legitimate power
   c. expert and referent power
   d. all of the above

7. The _____ model of leadership holds that leadership effectiveness is a function of the leader's style and the leadership setting.
   a. trait
   b. situational
   c. contingency
   d. group

8. Which of the following factors may lead to deindividuation?
   a. arousal
   b. anonymity
   c. diffusion of responsibility
   d. drug-induced alterations in consciousness
   e. all of the above

9. Research suggests that, compared to individual decisions, group discussion leads to _____ decisions.
   a. risky
   b. conservative
   c. extreme or polarized
   d. faster

10. Which of the following is a method for helping individuals avoid the tragedy of the commons?
    a. regulation of the resource
    b. increase in the size or the number of subgroups
    c. decrease in communication between parties
    d. all of the above

11. _____ are members of groups who are particularly influential and who act to guide, direct, and motivate the group to achieve its goals.
    a. Leaders
    b. Competitors
    c. Individualists
    d. Brainstormers

12. Social _____ processes occur when group discussion leads members to become aware of group norms.
    a. thinking
    b. comparison
    c. facilitation
    d. division

141

13. According to Janis, groups are most susceptible to groupthink when they
    a. are cohesive
    b. are isolated
    c. lack impartial leadership
    d. all of the above

14. The _____ Dilemma is a game in which two players simultaneously choose either a competitive or a cooperative response.
    a. Commons
    b. Social Trap
    c. Prisoner's
    d. Group

15. A mass psychogenic illness is more likely to occur
    a. with male executives
    b. in jobs that are exciting and different
    c. with stressed workers performing tedious work
    d. due to the flu than a cold

ANSWERS TO COMPLETION ITEMS

 1. group (568)
 2. activity; likability; task (570)
 3. presence; dominant (574-575)
 4. Brainstorming (582)
 5. task; socioemotional (592-593)
 6. processes (569)
 7. trap (605)
 8. Task specialists (589)
 9. polarization (584)
10. mind (587)

ANSWERS TO MATCHING QUESTIONS

1. b (577-578)
2. e (578)
3. c (578)
4. a (578-579)
5. g (596)
6. d (598-599)
7. f (585)

ANSWERS TO MULTIPLE CHOICE QUESTIONS

1. d (568)
2. a (572-575)
3. b (605)
4. b (570)
5. c (579-581)
6. d (590)
7. c (592)
8. e (596-601)
9. c (584)
10. a (607)
11. a (588)
12. b (584)
13. d (586-587)
14. c (602-605)
15. c (598-599)

CHAPTER 16

APPLYING SOCIAL PSYCHOLOGY

CHAPTER OUTLINE

I. <u>Introduction</u>

    A. Answering Social Questions
    B. Designing Social Interventions
    C. Evaluating Social Programs

II. <u>Social Psychological Factors in Health</u>

    A. Stress, Social Support, and Illness
       1. Stress and health
       2. Social support and health
    B. Personality, Health, and Illness
       1. Feelings of control
       2. Hardiness
       3. Optimism

III. <u>Using Social Psychology to Make People Healthier</u>

    A. Personal Control and Health
    B. Helplessness in the Elderly
    C. The Age of Prevention

IV. <u>Cultivating Our Garden</u>

V. <u>Summary</u>

VI. <u>Glossary</u>

LEARNING OBJECTIVES

After reading and studying Chapter 16, you should be able to answer the following questions.

1. What are the three ways that social psychologists apply their knowledge to real-life problems? (613-615)

2. What is stress and how is it measured? (616-620)

3. What is the relationship between stress and illness? (616-620)

4. How do we define and measure social support? What are the three broad varieties of social support? (620-623)

5. Is social support related to mortality, and if so how? (620-623)

6. What are some of the personality characteristics that are related to health and illness? (623-639)

7. How are feelings of control measured by psychologists? Does locus of control correlate with health and health-related behaviors? (623-625)

8. What are the three dimensions of the hardy personality? Does hardiness buffer the effects of high levels of stress on illness? (625-627)

9. How is optimism related to illness and health? (627-628)

10. How do social-psychological variables influence stress and its effects on health and illness? (628)

11. Summarize the relationship between Type A behavior and coronary heart disease. How is Type A and B behavior measured? (629-630)

12. Summarize some of the findings on the relationship between personal control and health. How is personal control related to learned helplessness? (631-632)

13. Describe the research findings on and implications of giving more personal responsibility to nursing home residents. (632-638)

14. Describe some social psychological processes that affect doctor-patient interactions. (634-635)

KEY TERMS TO KNOW

After reading and studying Chapter 16, you should be able to define or understand the following terms.

evaluation research (614-615)
stress (616)
Schedule of Recent Life Experiences (617-618)
Hassles Scale (617-619)
social support (620-623)
stress-buffering hypothesis (622-623)
locus of control (623-625)
Health Locus of Control Scale (624-625)
hardiness (625-627)
optimism (627-628)
Type A and B behavior patterns (629)
personal control (631-632)
learned helplessness (631-632)
preventative medicine (638-639)

COMPLETION ITEMS

Fill in the word(s) to complete each of the following statements. Check your responses against the correct answers at the end of this chapter.

1. _____ psychology is an optimistic field that assumes that social psychology can contribute to a better _____.

2. Hardiness comprises three components -- a sense of _____, _____ and _____ in life.

3. The _____ Locus of Control Scale measures the degree to which individuals feel in control of their health.

4. Individuals with high degrees of optimism report _____ physical illness and _____ physical well-being.

5. Experiments have shown that noxious stimuli, such as loud noises, are less stressful when subjects feel they can _____ them.

6. Cohen and McKay (1984) describe three broad varieties of social support: _____, _____, and _____.

7. The two leading causes of fatal cancers are _____ use and _____ habits.

8. People living in "total institutions" like mental hospitals often experience greatly reduced personal _____.

MATCHING TERMS AND CONCEPTS

Write the letter of the term or concept from below that best fits the following phrases or sentences. Check your responses against the correct answers at the end of this chapter.

___ 1. Research that measures the effectiveness of a social program or applied intervention

___ 2. External stimuli and the appraisal of external stimuli that lead to chronic arousal

___ 3. The degree to which individuals have a general expectation that successes and positive events will occur

___ 4. Individuals' perception that they are able to control aspects of their environment

___ 5. A list of everyday occurrences that people find to be annoying, irritating, or frustrating

___ 6. The comfort, assistance, and/or information one receives from others

a. personal control
b. evaluation research
c. Hassles Scale
d. stress
e. optimism
f. social support

MULTIPLE CHOICE QUESTIONS

Circle the one best answer to each question.
Check your responses against the correct answers
at the end of this chapter.

1. Which personality type is characterized by
   intense ambition, impatience, hostility, and
   a sense of time urgency?
   a. Type A   c. Type B
   b. hardy   d. none of the above

2. Which of the following is <u>not</u> one of the ways
   that social psychologist apply their
   knowledge to real-life problems?
   a. They attempt to answer social questions.
   b. They help design social interventions.
   c. They evaluate social programs.
   d. none of the above

3. According to research by Holmes and Rahe
   (1967), the most stressful life experience is
   a. divorce
   b. the death of a spouse
   c. being fired at work
   d. a jail term

4. A friend who cleans your house while you are
   in the hospital is providing _____
   social support.
   a. emotional   c. informational
   b. cognitive   d. tangible

5. According to Seligman (1975), when animals or
   people are repeatedly exposed to
   uncontrollable aversive events (like noise),
   they often show
   a. hardiness
   b. learned helplessness
   c. personal control
   d. optimism

6. Research by Rhodewalt and Smith suggests that _____ is the component of Type A behavior that is most linked to heart disease.
   a. impatience
   b. competitive drive
   c. hostility
   d. goal seeking

7. Research by Kobasa and associates (1982) found that managers who were _____ on stress and had a _____ degree of hardiness experienced the most illness.
   a. high; low
   b. high; high
   c. low; low
   d. low; high

8. The _____ hypothesis holds that social support many influence the development of illness and protect against the negative effects of stress.
   a. locus of control
   b. social support
   c. stress-buffering
   d. preventive medicine

9. Langer and Rodin (1976) demonstrated that nursing home residents who were assigned responsibility for everyday aspects of their life
   a. were less likely to participate in other scheduled activities
   b. were tired by the extra work and responsibility
   c. had a lower mortality rate 18 months later
   d. all of the above

10. Which of the following is not one of the eight main areas of stress in everyday life according to the Hassles Scale?
    a. time pressure hassles   c. work hassles
    b. recreational hassles   d. health hassles

ANSWERS TO COMPLETION ITEMS

1. Applied social; world (641)
2. control; commitment; challenge (625)
3. Health (624-625)
4. less; greater (627)
5. control (631)
6. tangible; informational; emotional (620)
7. tobacco; dietary or eating (639)
8. control (632)

ANSWERS TO MATCHING QUESTIONS

1. b (614)
2. d (616)
3. e (627)
4. a (631)
5. c (617)
6. f (620)

ANSWERS TO MULTIPLE CHOICE QUESTIONS

1. a (629)
2. d (613-615)
3. b (617-618)
4. d (620)
5. b (631-632)
6. c (630)
7. a (625-626)
8. c (622-623)
9. c (633-636)
10. b (617)